As a Christian committed to social j_____ there is little
more important than how we are raising and educating our children regarding their faith. David Csinos and Melvin Bray continue to do great work in
service to us all by assembling this thought-provoking and insightful collection of essays on the future of children's and youth ministry from some of this
field's leading thinkers and doers. I highly recommend this book to anyone
who cares about their kids and the future of Christianity – as this is what our
children represent.

Jim Wallis, author of *The UnCommon Good,*
president of Sojourners, and editor-in-chief
of *Sojourners* magazine

The rich diversity of perspectives in this second volume invite you to "meetup"
with a variety of people who believe that supporting the lives of faith of young
people is most important work. Come into their space, hear their stories, and
begin to re-imagine your ministry with children, youth, and their families.

Elizabeth F. Caldwell, Professor Emerita,
McCormick Theological Seminary,
Visiting Professor, Vanderbilt Divinity School

An amazing collection of compelling voices that calls us to the work of transforming the formational experiences of our children to birth life-long and life
giving faith. These luminous voices remind us that this is our work: handing
our children the promise and watching it enliven them.

Amy K. Butler, Senior Minister, The Riverside Church

I read this book with holy envy, wishing my two daughters had had an opportunity to receive the blessing of Faith Forward as they were growing up.
What a treasure this book is for parents, clergy, and educators today! Fresh faith
is here and she is beautiful.

Samir Selmanović, author, speaker, and leadership coach

I am grateful that I've been able to participate in Faith Forward since its inception. Dave Csinos and Melvin Bray are thinkers, conveners, curators, and friends. I love that they create space for conversation about new ideas. The environment they nurture isn't driven by an ideological agenda and makes me think of Aristotle's dictum, "It is the mark of an educated mind to be able to entertain a thought without accepting it." This book is filled with ingredients for new possibilities, concepts, and imagination for children's and youth ministry.

Mike King, President/CEO, Youthfront,
author of *Presence-Centered Youth Ministry*

This is a compelling collection of thoughts and practices for innovative ministry. This book is helping to forge the way for effective ministry in a new era.

Michael Novelli, author of *Shaped by the Story:*
Discover the Art of Bible Storying

Across the world, the church is struggling to engage with younger generations. *Faith Forward* enters the struggle and offers ways forward through the wisdom of theologians, practitioners, and church leaders. Don't read this book unless you are ready to hear afresh God's vision for children and youth in our churches – and are ready to take up the challenge!

Mary Hawes, National Going for Growth
(Children and Youth) Adviser, Church of England

Taken together, the collected voices of *Faith Forward* provide a rich stimulant to anyone – practitioners, teachers, parents, volunteers – seeking to engage new and innovative approaches to children's and youth ministry. All those wishing to steward the journey of young people toward a deeper, more meaningful experience of God will appreciate the power of this volume to challenge, inform, and inspire.

Richard DuBose, President,
Montreat Conference Center

Even better than Volume 1! The excitement, energy and innovation of Faith Forward gatherings have been made available in an easily accessible, eminently readable form. Arising from the curated conversations, nurtured spirits, and ministry experience of participants from around the globe, this book has a valuable role to play in challenging, and revolutionizing, faith formation practices with young people everywhere.

Chris Barnett, Children and Families Ministry Coordinator,
Centre for Theology and Ministry, Melbourne

Faith Forward
Volume 2

FAITH
FORWARD

VOLUME 2
Re-Imagining Children's and Youth Ministry

Edited by David M. Csinos & Melvin Bray
Foreword by Jennifer Knapp

CopperHouse

Editor: Michael Schwartzentruber
Cover: Mark Novelli, IMAGO
Interior : Cyrus Gandevia
Proofreader: Dianne Greenslade
Cover image: Shutterstock.com

CopperHouse is an imprint of Wood Lake Publishing, Inc. Wood Lake
Publishing acknowledges the financial support of the Government of
Canada through the Canada Book Fund (CBF) for its publishing activities.
Wood Lake Publishing also acknowledges the financial support of the
Province of British Columbia through the Book Publishing Tax Credit.

At Wood Lake Publishing, we practise what we publish, being guided by a concern for fairness, justice, and equal opportunity in all of our relationships with employees and customers. Wood Lake Publishing is committed to caring for the environment and all creation. Wood Lake Publishing recycles, reuses, and encourages readers to do the same. Resources are printed on 100% post-consumer recycled paper and more environmentally friendly groundwood papers (newsprint), whenever possible. A percentage of all profit is donated to charitable organizations.

Library and Archives Canada Cataloguing in Publication

Faith forward. Volume 2, Re-imagining children's and youth ministry
/ edited by David M. Csinos & Melvin Bray ; foreword by Jennifer Knapp.

Texts based on presentations made at the Faith Forward 2014 gathering
    held May 19-22, 2014, in Nashville, Tennessee.
Includes bibliographical references.
Issued in print and electronic formats.
ISBN 978-1-77064-799-2 (pbk.).--ISBN 978-1-77064-800-5 (html)

    1. Church work with children--Congresses. 2. Church work with
youth--Congresses. 3. Children--Religious life--Congresses. 4. Youth--
Religious life--Congresses. I. Csinos, David M., 1984-, editor II. Bray,
Melvin, editor III. Faith Forward (Conference) (2014 : Nashville, Tenn.)
IV. Title: Re-imagining children's and youth ministry.

BV4447.F353 2015   259'.2   C2015-901220-1
                                                             C2015-901221-X

Published by CopperHouse
An imprint of Wood Lake Publishing Inc.
485 Beaver Lake Road, Kelowna, BC, Canada, V4V 1S5
www.woodlakebooks.com
250.766.2778

Printing 10 9 8 7 6 5 4 3 2 1
Printed in Canada

For young people who had to give up religion in order to find a faith worth believing, and for the adults who inspire them.

Contents

MeetUp – Story

MeetUp – Rhythm

Acknowledgements

Faith Forward only exists through the dedication and support of those who share our mission: bringing together children's and youth ministry leaders for collaboration, resourcing, and inspiration toward innovative theology and practice. And it's no different for this book. We are grateful for the many people and organizations who have worked to make this book come to life.

First, we are grateful for those who served with us on the Faith Forward 2014 organizing team: Michael Novelli; Ivy Beckwith; Amy Butler; Danielle Shroyer; Kevin and Britta Alton; Lilly Lewin; Jenny Csinos; Amy Dolan; Mindi Godfrey; Aaron Niequist; the good folks at Imago led by Mark Novelli; and our host venues, Downtown Presbyterian Church, McKendree United Methodist Church, and Nashville Public Library. Thank you for all the sweat equity you have poured into our shared vision. There could not have been better companions in this adventure.

Wood Lake Publishing continues to be a tremendous supporter of Faith Forward and we are thankful for Patty Berube, Debbie MacDonald, Mike Schwartzentruber, and the whole team behind Wood Lake. Thank you for being our partners on the journey to create this book.

One of the things we love about Faith Forward is the opportunity to have meaningful conversations with the wide variety of ministry leaders and practitioners who join us for our gatherings. And the icing on the cake is the ongoing dialogue that continues in and through this book. Thank you to all of you who share your wisdom within these pages. You inspire us to re-imagine ministry, faith, and life.

Words are inadequate for expressing our gratefulness to those who have walked with us closest on this journey – our families. Thank you for giving us space to dedicate to this project, for being sounding boards for sharing ideas, and for holding us up along the way.

Finally, thank *you* for picking up this book and for being part of the MeetUp we have organized in the pages that follow. Together, we can walk toward brave new worlds with courage and hope, re-imagining ministry and faith with young disciples.

Foreword

As a young tomboy, I was introduced to Jesus while stuffed into an itchy pair of pantyhose and blisteringly tight patent leather shoes. Perhaps that was my grandmother's plan so that I might come to understand something of Christ's suffering?

I loathed the early Sunday morning classes, having had enough of learning during the week at school. Worse was the formal church service full of rituals and long-winded homilies I barely understood. For all I had ever been able to comprehend, church was the pursuit of "good" people and I was supposed to want to be one of them. I was supposed to find the joy of Christ sitting amongst all the blue-haired ladies and their stealthy dozing husbands. For me, there was more struggle than joy. In truth, it was all I could do to sit quietly, pinned down on a hard wooden pew. My only prayers were for a short sermon and a forthcoming reward of post-service potluck casseroles. With that inauspicious introduction to Christianity, it's a minor miracle that I've made it this far.

Highly recognized as a premier artist in the Christian Contemporary Music genre, **Jennifer Knapp** (jenniferknapp.com, @jennifer_knapp) chose to confront long-held speculation with a very public "coming out" in 2010. Her albums include *Set Me Free* and *Letting Go*, and she recently authored her first book, *Facing the Music*. Jennifer faces doubt with poise and tackles fear with candour, naturally opening the door to compassionate and constructive dialogue that affirms LGBT people in communities of faith.

I have, at times, described and criticized the church culture of my childhood as an experience of indoctrination. Though, if I borrow language from Brian McLaren, it might be more apt and decidedly less sinister to recognize my religious experience as an "inheritance"– an inheritance that has been prayerfully offered by my elders as an invitation into a rich, purpose-filled spiritual life. Even with the occasional baggage, or odd directions given in how to walk a path of faith, the gift has, ultimately, been a blessing. If ever I feel the need to analyze the methods or theology used by those who have paved my way, may I be humbly reminded that we all struggle to keep up with changing times at one point or another. The Christianity I saw as a child is undoubtedly different than what I see now as an adult. The test is to not judge it backward, but rather to learn from the experience and then, as best we can, pay it forward. For every parent, Sunday school teacher, and youth pastor, the challenge is ongoing: to share our faith with a youngster with relevance in the present while still providing room to grow. The question is, "How do we authentically bridge the modern needs, language, and culture gaps between one generation and the next?" And "How can we do so while honouring our past inheritance while moving forward in our faith?"

Apart from the unchanging gospel of Christ, the church of my early youth is nothing like the church I live in today. Not only has the dress code relaxed to T-shirts and jeans, we have mood lighting and PowerPoint presentations to go along with the sermons. More than that, our needs are different. We whisper less and talk more about all of life's demands – from the seen to the unseen. We are families going through divorce, having children, "coming out," and, sometimes, barely even clinging to the faith we first arrived with.

Our modern church is as loud and bold as the world that surrounds us. We have taken the invitation to faith and dared to run with it as far and wide as God will take us. We've graduated from WWJD bracelets and Ichthus bumper stickers to a genuine desire to live out grace. Our faith has reached into our politics, ethical consumer habits, workplace, and now in the desire to pass that faith onto the generations that follow us.

What, then, will we pass along?

It may be the ultimate ruse to think that we could ever teach faith or truly grant another person access to God, but what Faith Forward and the authors here hope to achieve is something altogether different from the Sunday school of decades gone by. The invitation is here to re-imagine sharing our Christian faith with our youth, beyond the trappings of mere religious culture and practice. It is an invitation to experience God, faith, and the extraordinary spiritual life. It is a daunting invitation because faith is a gift that cannot be taught. It must be given and received in order to succeed in its promise. Like all gifts, the joy is only made complete when one is able to recognize and claim that gift as one's own.

Introduction

Food, Fire, and Folk Songs

David M. Csinos and Melvin Bray

In the final chapter of the first Faith Forward book, esteemed religious educator John Westerhoff reminded us that faith is a gift, and that it is formed in communities. At the second gathering hosted by Faith Forward, which took place in Nashville, May 19– 22, 2014, hundreds of friends and conversation partners joined forces to share ideas and practices for how we can cultivate communities in which faith is formed in children and youth. But, in the process, we formed a community of faith, a community that called us to slow down and listen to the rhythm of our own faith lives, our own spirits, even as our main purpose was to talk about the faith of the young people with whom we minister.

The 2014 Faith Forward gathering was never supposed to happen. When we and our colleagues on the planning team organized our first gathering in 2012 (which was then called Children, Youth, and a New Kind of Christianity), we thought we were planning a one-time event (even though some of us suspected this wouldn't be the case). But shortly after returning to our homes, feedback from participants started pouring in faster than we could sift through it. We heard from ministry leaders who said that this event was the only place they'd been where they felt safe enough to talk about difficult issues and to ask questions that were controversial but incredibly important for the future of faith among young people. Others said that they were close to burnout and were set on quitting their ministry roles until they were inspired and enriched by others at the gathering. We all knew that this was not the end of our efforts. It was only the beginning.

We quickly got to work mapping our way forward. We formed an ecumenical organization called Faith Forward and began to lay plans for another gathering. Two years later, our dreams came to fruition with the 2014 Faith Forward gathering.

A sacred thing happened when we gathered at Downtown Presbyterian Church in Nashville – God breathed new life into us. God inspired us to see new visions and dream new dreams for what it means to walk with children and youth on the journey of following Jesus. It is our hope that this book will capture these dreams and visions as we seek to continue to join God in revolutionizing theologies and practices surrounding faith formation with young people.

Faith Forward has become a sort of MeetUp in the world of ministry with children and youth. Our gatherings are times and places where forward-thinking practitioners, theologians, and activists join together to network, resource, and inspire one another toward innovative theology and practice. And at our 2014 gathering, hundreds of leaders from around the world and spanning dozens of theological and denominational traditions joined forces in Nashville to re-imagine children's and youth ministry.

We imagine that this book is also a MeetUp of sorts. It is a venue in which friends old and new can encounter one another and share ideas and practices surrounding common interests, challenges, and calls. We have structured this book with this metaphor in mind.

Like any gathering of friends and colleagues, we begin our time by meeting in a common space – a coffee house, perhaps – to orient ourselves and talk about the experiences, issues, and visions we bring with us. So this book begins with two chapters – the first by Dave Csinos and Ivy Beckwith and the second by

Brian McLaren – that call us to remember what we bring to our time together and what we hope to accomplish through our re-imaginings.

From this initial gathering, we imagine walking together down the street to a home that a friend has opened to us, a more intimate place where we can explore, investigate, and experience ministry with children and youth. Each space in this home is hosted by guides and mentors who share their passions and visions with us.

At first we make our way to the kitchen, where we help prepare delicious food to nourish our bodies. We cut fresh, crisp vegetables, slice a couple loaves of warm bread, and pour hot cups of coffee and tea for one another. And as we sit around the kitchen table filling our plates and our stomachs, we enter into deep discussion with one another about our faith experiences, our personal beliefs, and why we care so deeply about ministry with young people. Here we are led by Andrew Root, Bonnie Miller-McLemore, and Kevin Alton, who give us food for thought as they help us reflect theologically on ministry with youth and children.

With our bellies filled with good food and our minds and hearts filled with good words, we notice what a beautiful evening it is and make our way outside. As we find a blanket, tree stump, or bench to sit on, someone lights a campfire at the centre of our circle and we begin sharing stories about our faith journeys and our efforts to nurture the faith journeys of our young friends. Here is where we meet Melvin Bray, Sandy Sasso, and Danielle Shroyer as they illuminate the formative power of stories, at times sharing some stories of their own. We also meet three poets – Constance Bynum, Niya McCray, and Romal Tune – who share stories of young people calling the church to meet them at the point of their need.

We become lost in our stories for some time, until someone remarks that the campfire we've gathered around reminds them of all the songs they sang with friends around past campfires. In a moment of stillness in our circle, we hear music playing faintly in the night and we head back to the house to investigate where it's coming from. We see a light on in the basement and head down the back stairs into a cozy den, where we are greeted with a warm smile and a tune played on an old, worn guitar. We squeeze in together and, in the warm glow of a few lamps, we create music together. Our song leaders in this space – Paul-André Durocher, Alaina Kleinbeck, Anne Wimberly, and Phyllis Tickle – impart to us the ways in which the rituals and practices that give life rhythm are catalysts for faith among those young disciples we accompany on the journey of faith.

Before we know it, our time together is over. We have one last drink, sing a song of benediction, and say "until next time" to old friends and new partners on our common quest.

The food is prepared. The fire is lit. The music is playing. God has sent each of us an invitation to this MeetUp. Come on in.

Chapter 1

Megachurches, Dark Nights, and Wonder-Bread Communion

Ivy Beckwith and David M. Csinos

When Faith Forward was born, we – along with rest of the Faith Forward team – dreamed of bringing together leaders in children's and youth ministry in order to equip, inspire, and resource one another as we re-imagine what it means to live in the way of

Ivy Beckwith is Faith Formation Team Leader for the United Church of Christ. She is a speaker, consultant, and author of several books, including *Children's Ministry in the Way of Jesus* (with David Csinos), *Postmodern Children's Ministry*, and *Formational Children's Ministry*. Ivy holds a Ph.D. in Religious Education and has held educational positions in churches in both the Midwest and on the East Coast of the United States.

David M. Csinos (davecsinos.com, @dcsinos) is founder and president of *Faith Forward* and author of several books and resources related to children, youth, and faith formation, including *Faith Forward* (with Melvin Bray), *Children's Ministry in the Way of Jesus* (with Ivy Beckwith), and *Children's Ministry that Fits*. Dave speaks internationally about innovative approaches to faith formation. He is a doctoral candidate in practical theology at Emmanuel College of Victoria University in the University of Toronto.

Jesus with young people. And as we've joined together for Faith Forward gatherings in 2012 and 2014, we've met hundreds of people who are experimenting with ministry with children and youth in thoughtful, creative, and innovative ways. In fact, when these leaders gather together, a space is curated in which ideas and practices can be generated and shared with one another. One of the most important ways this happens is by telling stories – stories of how we've rethought our theological assumptions and recast faith practices into the rhythm of our lives. So, with this in mind, we offer our stories of doubt, disillusionment, and hope on the journey to re-imagine ministry with children and youth.

Ivy's Story

I had reached the pinnacle of children's ministry. I was on staff at a large, growing mega-church with a celebrity senior pastor, 1,200 children on the rolls (800 or 900 would show up each Sunday), 550 volunteers, 600 kids in VBS each year, and another 200 children who would show up for mid-week programs. I was the administrator of a once-a-week school, concerning my days with curriculum, recruiting volunteers, training leaders and teachers, keeping track of supplies, interacting with parents, and negotiating working with a large staff of pastors, of whom I was the only woman. By the time I left this position, I had a staff team of five children's ministry associates that I was supervising. I did all this while blithely believing that everything I was doing would turn all these children into Christians. When I left that church staff, I was burned out. I could not handle one more recruiting season or one more teacher-training session.

I moved into the world of Sunday school curriculum publishing, working first in the area of sales and marketing and then making my way into editing. Once again, I felt like I'd made it –

at least in terms of the small world of children's ministry. All of a sudden, I was a workshop leader at Sunday school gatherings all over the country, and I was doing workshops at children's pastor conferences, hobnobbing with children's ministry royalty.

But as I worked at developing new children's ministry resources and as my view of what was happening in churches across the country broadened, I began to have an uneasy feeling that mainstream children's ministry was losing its way. There seemed to be too much emphasis on fun, on making church be something other than church. And it seemed as though our dependence on a schooling model was not the best way to spiritually form our children. I felt the church had allowed parents to abdicate their responsibility for creating a family faith identity by telling families that we who are children's and youth ministry professionals can do it better than they can.

This coincided with my developing interest in the postmodern cultural shift. I began to read everything I could get my hands on, especially material about the church and its response to postmodernism. I became convinced that the church needed to face this issue head on and embrace it – not run away from it or attempt to combat it. So I decided to go back into local church children's ministry.

This decision – which was closely followed by a national tragedy – would prove to be life-altering and faith-altering for me. In 2000, I moved from California back to my home in Minnesota and joined a theologically moderate church. Here I was plunged into the world of emerging churches courtesy of some old friends, some new friends, and my new church's youth pastor, and I was encouraged by the senior minister to rethink how this church thought about and engaged in children's ministry.

I pulled two books off my office bookshelf: *A Theology of Children's Ministry* by Larry Richards, and *Will Our Children Have Faith?* by John Westerhoff. Both books, while written from seemingly opposite ends of the theological spectrum, had very similar messages. The authors agreed that approaches to children's ministry based on a formal schooling-instructional model are no way to help children live in the way of Jesus. Both agreed that church faith formation ministries tend to underestimate the role of the family in a child's spiritual nurture and fail to challenge families to live in the way of Jesus, as models to their children. And both agreed on the importance of the faith community, particularly intergenerational relationships in the faith formation of the church's children.

So I decided to create a way of doing children's ministry that emphasized these principles, adding the idea of corporate worship as a vehicle for spiritual transformation. As I was beginning to enact this change in the way my church did children's ministry, 9/11 happened. This horrible tragedy threw me into a spiritual tailspin. It called into question everything I believed about God and faith. I entered a "dark night of the soul." I couldn't pray. But I was an ordained minister serving a church, so I muddled through. Somewhere deep inside of me, I knew I still wanted to be a person of faith, but I also knew that what that would look like would be vastly different from what it had looked like in the past.

This was the time when my emerging church connections proved to be personally invaluable. I've heard people who walked down this path say over and over again, "Emergent saved my life" – and I am one of those people. My friends and the ideas we explored during the first half of the first decade of the 21st century showed me a new way of being a person of faith.

I wish I could say that as I emerged from that "dark night" I created a way of doing children's ministry in which families nurture their children, intergenerational relationships flourish, and the secret of pan-generational worship is unlocked. While some of these things happened to a particular degree, my tenure at the church in Minnesota ended with my leaving under less-than-optimal circumstances.

I left congregational ministry for a while, supporting myself through executive recruiting, book writing, and speaking engagements. But I continued to think about new faith formation practices with children and youth. In 2006, I was invited to become the Minister to Children and Families at the Congregational Church of New Canaan, Connecticut. Here, thanks to a large endowment, I was allowed to experiment with intergenerational worship, experiential age-appropriate worship, a tiny formational weekday preschool, and new ways of engaging children in the biblical narrative.

During a late night conversation at the first Faith Forward gathering, back in 2012, someone asked me what children's ministry looks like in my congregation. I was serving a Presbyterian church in Manhattan at the time. Questions like this strike fear into me, because while I work hard to align the practical work of children's and youth ministry with my philosophical and theological beliefs – those things that I write and speak about – people who walk into that building at Broadway and 73rd Street might not see anything that looks very different from the large Presbyterian churches across the park. As I strove to respond to that question, I knew I wasn't there yet – I knew that the way I engage in practical ministry has yet to fully incarnate my theological views. But I also knew that I was doing countless little things that were different, new, and innovative – they weren't enough, but I was making progress.

Dave's Story

I was born into a practicing Roman Catholic family and grew up as a member of a local parish that blended social justice, spirituality, and music into a potent elixir for encountering God in very real ways. Throughout my childhood and teen years, my faith was formed through practices of prayer, worship, and contemplation that allowed me to have first-hand experiences with God; a God that I came to know through these encounters as loving, beautiful, and mysterious. I was, in many ways, a poster child for this congregation, showing the power of enculturation as the six-year-old version of myself played Mass at a desk-turned-altar in my bedroom – complete with Communion hosts cut out of a flattened slice of Wonder bread.

But the old real estate adage rang true as I left this parish in northern Ontario to pursue my undergraduate degree 500 kilometres south – location, location, location. For the first time in my life, I found myself in a context that wasn't largely characterized by the Catholicism of that mining community in which I was raised. The friends I made at university possessed theological lenses and denominational ties that I had only heard about, but never really understood. As we got to know one another, we shared our faith with one another. But since my faith was largely built on encounters with God that I had not always shared with others, I struggled to express my faith to these new friends in words, to respond to theological questions that I had never really stopped to ask. As much as I had encountered God during childhood and adolescence, I came to realize that I had never constructed a cogent theological understanding of this God and what it really means to be a follower of Jesus in my daily life.

Intrigued by my friends' articulate theological understandings and somewhat ashamed at my lack thereof, my faith life shifted from one end of the spectrum to the other, as I made an about-face away from experience and toward theological reasoning. My collection of theological books went from the lone high school religion textbook that I forgot to give back at the end of the year (sorry, Mrs. Scappatura) to shelves filled with the words of theologians and apologists who explicated Christianity and presented messages of salvation and faith in ways that seemed to make some sort of internal sense. And since I also felt called to ministry with young people, I surrounded myself with popular books offering appealing models for children's and youth ministry.

The next year or two was a sort of honeymoon period in my spiritual life, a time when I was on fire for God in new and exciting ways as I dove into life within a local evangelical congregation. But this honeymoon gave way to a rocky marriage of faith. The fairly conservative and simplistic theology that initially seemed to make so much sense had become an overbearing spouse, squashing the life out of the experiences of God that first formed my faith as a child and adolescent. These experiences had led me to know God as loving and caring. But this newfound theology made God seem wrathful and angry. The faith of my younger years was enlivened by mystery and wonder. This new theology seemed to fit God into a neat and easy-to-understand box – a box that no one would open on Christmas day if they could avoid it.

Don't get me wrong – this faith community was a formative influence on my faith, helping me to think theologically and see the Holy Spirit as active in every aspect of my life. But I wondered, did the dissonance between this theology and the experiences of God I had had in my younger years mean that these experiences weren't real? Fearful that the answer to this question would be yes, I just kept my head down and listened to the dominating voice.

After completing my undergraduate degree, I entered grad school at McMaster Divinity College, where my call to minister with youth and children evolved into a keen interest in the spiritual lives of young people. I bought another bookshelf and filled it with volumes about children's spirituality and adolescent development, books that I read and reread in order to gain insight into how I could help fan the spiritual flame in the young people with whom I was ministering during my day job as a part-time children's pastor.

During the summer after my first year at McMaster, I jumped at an opportunity to travel to Wheaton College Graduate School for a course on researching children's spirituality. During the first day in this intensive course, the professors asked all of us in the class to share a moment from our childhood that stood out as a spiritual experience. As we sat in a circle sharing these experiences, I struggled to come up with something to say. Deep down, I knew that I had had many God moments that were worth sharing. But the theological views I'd learned after moving away from home to attend university had pushed these moments to the periphery of my mind because the messages these experiences imparted about who God is and how to follow Jesus conflicted with those I had read about in my journey into evangelical Christianity. It was at this moment that I realized that the marriage between this newfound theology and my experiences as a young person was over – if it ever existed in the first place. For too long, certain theological views had drowned out the God-moments of my youth, telling me that they were not real because they didn't line up with the beliefs I had been taught in my explorations in evangelical Christianity.

I suddenly longed to be wrapped in mystery again. So I did what many people do during moments of existential crisis – I dug down deep and rediscovered the approach to a life of faith that had planted roots in my younger years. Free from a theology that stamped out my early experiences of God, I set out on a journey to rediscover those moments in my childhood and adolescence when God broke into my life through mystery, awe, and wonder. And as I reflected on these moments – a practice that I overlooked as a child and teen – I came to see that I didn't need an outside voice to infuse theological significance into them. These God moments were pregnant with theological meaning that, when birthed through ongoing reflection, spread into every corner of my theological imagination. It was in rediscovering the in-breaking of God in my childhood and teenage self that my understandings of who God is and what it means to follow Jesus took shape in ways that I could truly affirm – not just in my mind, but in my heart, my soul, and my strength as well.

As God continues to break into the rhythm of my life – often in unexpected ways – my journey of theological understanding continues and grows. In the end, it was in going back to that makeshift altar with Wonder bread Communion that my faith was saved.

Crowdsourcing a Revolution

We share these stories as a way of framing how we got to where we are as followers of Jesus and as leaders in ministry with young people. We imagine that some elements of these stories are similar to your stories and that some are different. But we share them because we believe that a dramatic re-imagining of children's and youth ministry begins with each one of the stories that we bring with us, tucked under our arms. Embedded in these stories is everything we need to bring about a revolutionary, all-encompassing shift in what it means to minister with youth and children.

As you move through this book, stop to think about your story. Write it down. Rewrite it. Share it with a friend or colleague. How did you get to where you are? What are you doing to nurture faith in youth and children?

As we all join together, we crowdsource our re-imaginings of children's and youth ministry in the way of Jesus. May our imaginations run away with us as we dream about what could be in our churches, families, and communities – and wherever else God calls us to nurture faith in children and youth.

Chapter 2

Launching a Revolution

Brian D. McLaren

- Blue metal folding chairs
- Bible memorization – being sure to say the reference before and after reciting the scripture, word perfect, of course
- "Sword drills" – where the teacher would shout out a Bible reference, say Exodus 19:6, and the first person to find it, stand, and read it aloud, would win
- Singing "Noah and the Arky Arky," "I've Got the Joy, Joy, Joy, Joy," "The B-I-B-L-E," and lots of songs about heaven
- Arts and crafts that, without the omnipresent popsicle sticks and macaroni, would have been limited to crayons, paper, and glue
- Bible storybooks in which Jesus always looked strangely Norwegian, amid a sea of decidedly Dutch kin
- Nightmare scenarios of getting hit by a train right after

Brian D. McLaren (brianmclaren.net, @brianmclaren) is an author, speaker, activist, and public theologian. He is a popular conference speaker and a frequent guest lecturer for denominational and ecumenical leadership gatherings in the U.S. and internationally. Brian's writing spans over a dozen books, including *We Make the Road by Walking*; *Why Did Jesus, Moses, the Buddha, and Mohammed Cross the Road?*; A New Kind of Christian trilogy; and *A Generous Orthodoxy*.

deciding to wait until tomorrow to say the "sinner's prayer" and "accept Jesus as your personal Lord and Saviour"
- Nightmare scenarios of coming home after school only to discover the Rapture has happened and your mother and father have been taken…and you have been LEFT BEHIND
- Compound nightmare scenarios described around blazing campfires at summer camp involving what happens to children who don't say "the sinner's prayer," who get LEFT BEHIND, and who never "accept Jesus as their personal Lord and Saviour"
- Flannelgraph, the true precursor to the Internet
- *Cold* blue metal folding chairs

People of my generation (the infamous Baby Boomers) who attended Sunday school and youth group often share memories like these. There are other memories we likely hold in common as well:
- Kind teachers and leaders who volunteered to try to teach squirmy kids and too-cool-for-Sunday-school teens week after week
- The chance to sing and make music – sometimes beautiful songs
- Exposure to the Bible and its promises of a life worth living, eternally
- Lessons about missionaries who did good work around the world – which included elementary instruction about geography and world affairs
- The conviction that there is such a thing as right and wrong, and that the difference really matters

- Experiences of getting out to sing Christmas carols at senior care facilities, prisons, and hospitals and other experiences raising money or food or doing good on behalf of others that students may not have otherwise had

Whenever I recall memories like these, I am deeply grateful that my parents made sure I was in Sunday school every week of my childhood, except those where I had a fever of over 100 degrees. The benefits far outweighed the liabilities.

A Universal Curriculum

It is amazing that persons from far and wide, separated by miles, ethnicities, and denominational distinctives could end up with such similar memories of childhood and adolescence. When I compare notes with other Sunday school veterans across the world, I'm led to think there must have been something called *The Universal Unwritten Sunday School Curriculum* that included sentiments like these:

1. **We want you to be a good child and churchgoer.** "Good little boys and girls," we learned, obey their parents and go to church.
2. **To be a Christian is to believe certain teachings.** The teachings varied from denomination to denomination. For example, with Southern Baptists, Assemblies of God, and Roman Catholics, knowing which stood for believers' baptism by full immersion, and which stood for speaking in tongues, and which stood for transubstantiation. But all agreed that Christian identity is related to a list of timeless teachings.

3. **We (the church) are here to teach the correct interpretation of the Bible.** Since denominations were legitimized by their correct interpretation, kids and teens learned why their denomination had it right and the other ones didn't.

4. **Jesus told us how to be nice, how to be successful, and how to go to heaven.** Sunday schools seemed to be unquestionably pro-Jesus. And in my context of the U.S., Jesus was unquestionably pro-American, pro-free-enterprise, pro-social-advancement, pro-nice, and pro-heaven.

5. **Because God is watching, you should be very careful (and afraid).** Most of us gained the sense that God was like a 24/7 universal CCTV system that could catch us doing wrong anywhere, including in our own heads. Since we all knew we had done terrible, damnable sins – from letting Billy McCarthy copy our math homework to urinating in the woods – this caused us considerable anxiety.

6. **We are sinners and need forgiveness.** Otherwise, we might be LEFT BEHIND…or something worse.

7. **You love God by being a good child and churchgoer.** There was a wonderful feedback loop that always brought us back to certain fixed essentials: *be good and go to church.*

There is a lot of good in this unwritten curriculum, not the least of which is that it gives a good reason for the whole church enterprise to continue existing. But based on the number of my peers and their children and their children's children who have dropped out of church since Sunday school, it might be time to question whether the unwritten curriculum gave a *good enough reason* for the whole church enterprise to continue existing.

Making a U-Turn

In my chapter in the first *Faith Forward* book, I included a quote often credited to organizational consultant Otto Scharmer. I share it again in this chapter because it remains as pertinent today – if not more pertinent – than it was two years ago: "What's missing today is a high-quality discourse on rethinking the design and evolution of the entire system from scratch." By the entire system, Scharmer means the whole of our society, including education, communication, government, the global economy – everything. And that, I think, applies to the whole church system as well, from Sunday school soup to seminary nuts.

This radical rethinking has been going on for quite some time. Consider, for example, these words from the brilliant Catholic missiologist Vincent Donovan, in his book *The Church in the Midst of Creation*:

> We can imagine that we are the sole possessors of the truth, that we have a monopoly on the truth, that we have no need of dialogue, no need of mutual fecundation and interpenetration with the non-Christian cultures that surround us, the Hindu, Buddhist, Islamic, traditional-religious, Marxist, scientific-technological cultures that make up our world...
>
> We can refuse to admit that we must commit ourselves to an exploration and discovery of a form of the church and its ministry and sacraments, a form of Christianity and of Christ, that we have not known.
>
> We can refuse to do all this, of course, but if we do refuse, we have to ask whether we, the current bearers of the Christian message, will not die and pass from history, just as surely as did the Judeo-Christians, or later, the African Christians of Augustine's time. They, too, had their day in the sun.[1]

Donovan decries what he called the "standardization" of ministry, where the principles of mass production that worked in making cars and plastic gizmos were assumed to be the ideal method for producing priests, pastors, and Christians: "standardized seminaries, priest factories, turned out identical products – standardized priests... Those who had resisted the standardized molding during the time of training were eliminated along the way – like defective products being pulled off the assembly line" (p. 40). He goes on to argue that the assembly line approach, which is meant to guarantee a product of good quality, "also does away with products that are superior.... The Industrial Revolution is dying in Western Europe and America, and so are its seminaries. The Industrial Revolution is just reaching the third world, and its seminaries are flourishing" (p. 40).

Along with standardization, he saw church leaders uncritically accepting other techniques of the industrial era: specialization, centralization (of power), concentration (people "processed" in large numbers), and maximalization (bigger is better). The results, he insisted, were not good. Christianity had been reduced to something as predictable as a McDonald's hamburger: "There was nothing further, nothing new...to say about Christ. [Industrialized Christianity] had said everything it could. All that was left were countless, spiritless repetitions and memorizations of the repetitions" (p. 54).

If Donovan's diagnosis is correct, then Scharmer's prescription is exactly what we need. We need to go through a U-shaped process of descent, quiet, and rebirth. We need to go through a process of letting go, letting be, and letting come in order to rethink the entire system from scratch.

Toward a New Curriculum

I know many people who have been experiencing this process, and those of us who join together at Faith Forward gatherings are among this group. While we've made progress, we have much work left to do. Nonetheless, certain things are becoming clear – among them, that the old universal unwritten Sunday school curriculum needs to be scrapped, and in its place perhaps something like the following would emerge.

Perhaps the primary goal of Christian children's and youth ministry would be *to help young people become life-long followers of God in the way of Jesus.* What matters, we are beginning to realize, is not mere attendance at weekly gatherings or membership in a religious institution, but rather a radical identity formation: in union/communion with God, as a learner/follower/disciple of Jesus who intends to keep learning/following/growing through all of life's stages. If we could help children and youth immerse and confirm their personal identity in this grand identity by the time they are young adults, we would be doing an amazing job.

With the focus off attendance and back on following, those of us walking this path have begun to redefine what it means for us to continue to identify as Christian. As we have come to understand it, *to be a Christian is to join Jesus in seeking justice for all, peace for all, and joy for all.* Teachings and beliefs are, indeed, important, but not as litmus tests or ends in themselves. Rather, appropriate beliefs, honestly held, prepare us to join in the mission/kingdom/reign of God, seeking the common good. If we can equip children and youth with the basic skills to live with this sense of purpose, priority, and mission, we are making a needed contribution. They will become a new generation of contemplative activists and reflective practitioners united in their desire to become truly Christ-like people.

To follow Jesus, we need to keep at the forefront of our minds that *Jesus gave us good news of a better way to be human, individually and collectively.* Jesus must become more important than before, but not merely as a solution to "the sin problem" or as a ticket-provider on the train to heaven. If we help children and youth discover a grander, more compelling, more coherent, and more demanding Christology, we will help them be human in a world of violence, war, conflict, hatred, weapons of mass destruction, religious hostility, global climate change, overconsumption, toxification, ecological destruction, greed, sea level rise, extinction of species, soil depletion, waste, poverty, mass migration, the 1% vs. the 99%, the growing gap between elites and masses, bought elections, political corruption, unaccountable corporations, vulnerable minorities...and majorities.

In a world such as this, imagination is more important than ever. And we need to help young people bring their imaginations to the quests to know God, for *God is greater than anyone can explain or imagine.* The Bible is indeed important, but not as a textbook that defines and reduces God to a certain formula or equation. Rather, the Bible presents key moments in humanity's attempts to grapple with our shared experience of God, the living God who can never be reduced to stone idol, conceptual formula, or human equation. If we can help children and youth experience, cultivate, and thirst for this holy awe and reverence in the presence of God, the universe will open up to be for them what it was for the psalmist – a declaration of the glory of God.

And when young people approach God with awe and imagination, they can do so knowing that *because God loves – and likes! – us perfectly, we don't have to be afraid.* The old fear-based system must be left behind, but we can't simply leave a vacuum in its place. Rather, we must help children and youth inhabit a universe that is ruled by love, a universe in which they are truly loved *and liked* by the Creator who is also their Companion and Friend. If we help them see themselves in God's circle of affection, along with every other human being – and with all creation whether animate or inanimate – we will give them a confidence, humility, and sense of connection that will empower them as no generation of Christians has ever been empowered.

When young people know deep within their bones that God not only loves them, but likes them too, then they can follow Jesus knowing that, although they will make mistakes, God still likes them. After all, *we all make mistakes, God forgives, and we can learn from our mistakes.* It is important to teach children and youth the categories of right and wrong, but right and wrong are far more than items on a checklist that a Santa-Claus-like God checks twice to determine one's niceness or naughtiness quotient. If we help children and youth think about actions and their consequences, short and long term, intended and unintended, and if we help children and youth understand how their actions affect others, and if we help them learn to process their mistakes in an environment of wisdom-seeking and grace, then we can build in them a conscience that will serve them well in a life of Christian service.

This conscience – this sense of purpose and action and consequences – can guide young people in how they live in the world, for *loving God means loving all creation with God, and the church exists to organize us for that purpose.* In a time of social conflict and impending environmental catastrophe, we must help students integrate love for God with love for neighbour, stranger, other, enemy, outsider, outcast, *and environment.* If our children and youth grow up with love as the unifying principle of life, we have prepared them well for life in the Spirit. And if they experience the church as a community that actually organizes itself to be and practise this loving presence in the world, they will have good reason to be enthusiastic church-people throughout their lives, infusing this vision in their children and grandchildren as well.

Rummage Sale Stories

This kind of curriculum will require a major "rummage sale," as Phyllis Tickle calls it.[2] As I've detailed in many of my books, we'll need to purge the "six-lined narrative" and replace it with "3-D story space."[3] We'll need to get a strong sense of the spacious biblical narrative, the story of the universe as God's creative endeavour into which we are invited as junior partners.[4] And within that story space, we'll need to find new ways to teach individual episodes of that story so that they are not abused in the future for violent and harmful purposes as they have been in the past. This kind of *conversational* storytelling might look something like this:

- Telling the story of David and Goliath in a way that includes the story of David committing violence in God's name *in conversation with* the story of David not being allowed to build the temple because he was a man of bloodshed.
- Telling the story of Noah's flood in a way in which God is depicted as violent, short-sighted, and indiscriminate in decreeing death by drowning nearly all earth's inhabitants *in conversation with* the story of the Exodus, where it is Pharaoh who drowns people and God who saves.
- Telling the story of the evil Egyptian slavemasters in Exodus *in conversation with* the story of Hagar, in which an Egyptian and her son are the slave and the victim of mistreatment, and placing these stories *in conversation with* the story of Solomon who used slave labour to build the temple.

- Telling the story of Joshua ordering the slaughter of Canaanites in God's name *in conversation with* the story of Jesus healing a Canaanite girl and then replicating a feeding and healing miracle for her Gentile neighbours.
- Telling the story of Ezra commanding men to divorce their "foreign wives" *in conversation with* the story of Ruth, in which it is a foreign wife who becomes the grandmother to King David. And using the story of Naomi and Ruth's quiet dignity to counter the ugliness of the men who fill the latter chapters of Judges doing "what is right in their own eyes."
- Telling the story of Elijah calling down fire on the prophets of Baal *in conversation with* Jesus who rebuked his disciples when they advocated the same behaviour, to which Jesus replied, "You do not know what spirit you are of."
- Telling the stories of Jacob and Esau *in conversation with* Jesus' parable of the prodigal son, where the father acts like Esau, the supposedly disfavoured son, in showing grace.

In all these ways and more, I believe that Christian educators – Sunday school teachers, youth workers, summer camp leaders, and others who focus on the spiritual formation of children and youth – can become the architects of a spiritual revolution that will not only rock the church (which needs some rocking), but also bring profound and needed change to the world.

Such a revolution is needed. But it won't be easy. Religious institutions do not typically welcome these kinds of changes, as Fr. Vincent Donovan explained:

Religion is our own creation. Its horizons are necessarily limited to our horizons. Since it is our creation it will serve us. In a time of social, political, and economic upheaval, we look to it as that one, solid, taken-for-granted basis to our lives. It leads us to cling to the forms and structures with which we are familiar and which we have found comforting. At the dying of an age and the birth of a new one, religion will be in the forefront of those institutions clinging desperately to that immovable rock of unanalyzed assumptions.[5]

But this is not the last word. God's word can break through even the most entrenched of religious institutions. As Donovan continues, "revelation shatters that rock, disturbs our horizons, presents a God who is not like us at all, a destabilizing and surprising God who cannot be used to justify all our projects; instead, One who asks us questions we do not want to hear."[6] It was for this reason that Fr. Donovan issued this bold challenge:

Never accept and be content with unanalyzed assumptions, assumptions about the work, about the people, about the church or Christianity. Never be afraid to ask questions about the work we have inherited or the work we are doing. There is no question that should not be asked or that is outlawed. The day we are completely satisfied with what we have been doing; the day we have found the perfect, unchangeable system of work, the perfect answer, never in need of being corrected again, on that day we will know that we are wrong, that we have made the greatest mistake of all.[7]

I know that children's and youth ministry leaders – Sunday School teachers seated on blue metal folding chairs, armed with popsicle sticks and macaroni (or videos and PowerPoint); and youth workers sitting on hand-me-down couches, armed with pizza and a student Bible – may not seem likely candidates for architects of a spiritual revolution. But aren't unlikely candidates at the front of almost all successful revolutions?

---

[1] Vincent J. Donovan, *The Church in the Midst of Creation* (Maryknoll, NY: Orbis, 1989), 20–21.

[2] Phyllis Tickle, *The Great Emergence: How Christianity Is Changing and Why* (Grand Rapids: Baker, 2008/2012).

[3] See especially Brian D. McLaren, *A New Kind of Christianity: Ten Questions That Are Transforming the Faith* (New York: HarperOne, 2010).

[4] See especially Brian D. McLaren, *The Story We Find Ourselves In: Further Adventures of a New Kind of Christian* (San Francisco: Jossey-Bass, 2003) and Brian D. McLaren, *We Make the Road by Walking: A Year-Long Quest for Spiritual Formation, Reorientation, and Activation* (New York: Jericho, 2014).

[5] Donovan, *The Church in the Midst of Creation*, 90.

[6] Ibid.

[7] Vincent J. Donovan, *Christianity Rediscovered* (Chicago: Fides/Claretian, 1978), 146.

MeetUp

Theology

Chapter 3

Theology Isn't Enough: Bonhoeffer, Dead Dogs, and a Ten-Year-Old's Tears[1]

Andrew Root

A few months ago, a very nice person approached me and thanked me for writing my book *The Theological Turn in Youth Ministry*. I was moved by these kind words. Keeping the conversation going, the person then said, "I was thankful for the book because I've been saying for years that we just need to get kids to read Paul Tillich." I stopped for a second, assuming the person was kidding. But inside the awkward few seconds of silence that followed, it became clear that there was no jest in these remarks. So I asked, "Why Tillich?" Confidently the person responded, "Because kids need theology!"

A number of thoughts ran around my head. The one most clearly tormenting me was, "And why do you think young

Andrew Root (andrewroot.org, @RootAndrew) is Olson Baalson Associate Professor of Youth and Family Ministry at Luther Seminary. He is the author of many books, including *Bonhoeffer as Youth Worker, Christopraxis, The Relational Pastor,* and *The Theological Turn in Youth Ministry* (with Kenda Creasy Dean). He lives in St. Paul, Minnesota, with his wife Kara, two children, Owen and Maisy, and their two dogs, Kirby and Kimmel.

people need theology?" Before the question could escape my mouth, I swallowed it, assuming it was rude, or at least odd, for the author of *The Theological Turn* to question the need for theology. Yet my own question continued to haunt me. Here I was having written a handful of books with titles like *The Theological Turn in Youth Ministry* and also *Taking Theology to Youth Ministry* and *Taking the Cross to Youth Ministry*. But I still wanted to ask, why do young people need theology at all?

I pondered the question for weeks, finally coming to the answer, ironically, not in reading Paul Tillich but in reading Dietrich Bonhoeffer. I came to the answer that young people don't need theology at all! I'll say this again because it may seem counterintuitive: *I don't think young people need theology.*

It hurts me to say that because I actually love theology; I love reading it and discussing it. But in the end I'm not sure *knowing* theology and all its doctrines will help young people follow Jesus; I'm not sure theology *alone* makes much of a difference in the practice of ministry. A turn to theology in youth ministry risks losing the lived and concrete experience of young people by bulldozing their questions, fears, and joys for information.

I think the kind person who complimented *The Theological Turn* had misread the title. It isn't *The "Theology" Turn in Youth Ministry*, but rather *The "Theological" Turn...*, and while at first glance these words seem to be synonymous, I see them as quite different.

A youth ministry that turns to *theology* seeks to move young people into forms of formal knowledge (to assimilate to the doctrinal). A youth ministry that turns to the *theological* seeks to share in the concrete and lived experience of young people as the very place to share in the act and being of God. The goal of a "theology turn" in youth ministry is to get kids to know information;

a "theological turn" in youth ministry seeks to minister to the concrete humanity of young people, seeking for God's action in and through their experience.

Yet I'm sure as you read this you're thinking, "Okay, but what does that actually look like? What do you mean?" Let me provide an example from the life of one of greatest theologians of the 20th century, Dietrich Bonhoeffer.

It is often overlooked that Bonhoeffer was not only one of the most talented students of theology in the 20th century, but he was also a youth worker. The entire ministry of Bonhoeffer between 1925 and 1939 (until WWII started) was with either children or youth.

In 1928, at the age of 22, with a completed PhD in theology in his back pocket, Bonhoeffer went on internship in Barcelona. Within weeks he revamped the Sunday school and started a youth group. An encounter he had a few months later with one of these young people, a 10-year-old boy, illustrates beautifully the difference between *theology* and the *theological*.[2]

One morning, a boy came to see Bonhoeffer. Dietrich had requested something from the boy's parents, and, as the boy arrives, Bonhoeffer becomes attuned to him, sensing that there is something wrong, as the usually cheerful boy seems out of sorts. The *theological* in youth ministry often has its impetus not in the formal but in the encounter of the experiential. Bonhoeffer has not organized a formal time of pastoral care, nor is he looking to teach the boy theology. Rather, as minister, he seeks to attune himself to the young person enough to seek the boy out, to ask the boy to speak of his experience.

This attunement shows the depth of Bonhoeffer's gifts for youth ministry. He does not see a one-dimensional child with flat and stupid concerns. Rather, Bonhoeffer contends that there is theological depth in the very concrete and lived experience of the boy – and his tears witness to it. Bonhoeffer is drawn into the boy's humanity, understanding that when this young person speaks of his experience it will come to Bonhoeffer with theological depth. As Bonhoeffer invites the boy to speak, it eventually comes out, the tears flowing. Bonhoeffer hears through the gasps of sobs as the boy repeats, "Mr. Wolf is dead. Mr. Wolf is dead."

Bonhoeffer dwells deeply in the boy's suffering, sharing it by experiencing the loss the boy must feel over his dead dog, Mr. Wolf; he writes a letter to his brother-in-law Walter Dress about this experience, telling him about the boy's deep emotional attachment to the dog. Bonhoeffer stands as the boy's place-sharer, inviting the boy to narrate his experience, to tell him how it was that the boy loved the dog and how the dog awoke him in the morning, playing with him all day.

As Bonhoeffer sits with the boy, the boy's sobbing is muted by the arrival of the theological; it wells up in him as his heavy experience is shared by another. Bonhoeffer stands neck-deep in the boy's experience. Having this experience shared by Bonhoeffer, the boy says, "But I know he is not dead at all!" – the theological has arrived. The boy uses what he has heard other boys say about death in religion class, what his teacher has responded about heaven, and constructs his theory of hope that he will again see his beloved dog, Mr. Wolf. The boy then directly addresses Bonhoeffer, looking for an answer; seeking confirmation from his pastor of his theory, the boy says, "But tell me now, will I see Mr. Wolf again? He's certainly in heaven."

Now Bonhoeffer's place-sharing leads to the impulse of confession and proclamation. Bonhoeffer did not sit with the boy and think, *the boy is weak; it is now time to convert him*. Rather,

Bonhoeffer just shares in the boy's experience, embracing him, patient and present in every tear. But now that the boy's person has been joined, he seeks clarity. The boy seeks to offer his conception of what is real through his experience; he loved Mr. Wolf, so Mr. Wolf is in heaven, right? The theological bursts forth from within the experiential, growing from the fertile soil of shared humanity through the action of ministry.

What is Bonhoeffer to say? He is stuck between theology and the theological. He perceives that the boy wants a yes or no answer. He knows that it is ministerial malpractice to not give an answer, to somehow drown the boy's questions in Socratic methods of avoidance, offering the boy's direct question only the answer of another question that gets him off the hook. The boy has shared his experience and now seeks to make sense of it; he seeks the *theological*, and the heavy stone of *theology* that may give the right *dogmatic* answer, but that takes no concern for the stained cheeks of the boy, will not do.

Bonhoeffer confesses in his letter to Walter Dress that children's and youth ministry is a deep and challenging locale in which to do the *theological*. He explains to Dress how he struggled with what to say, forced, through this experience, to think deeply. And like so many of us in youth ministry, he explains at the end of the letter that he felt small next to the significance of the boy's deep theological question. Bonhoeffer never doubted himself in defense of his dissertation, but in the shadow of the ten-year-old's cosmic question, raised by the lived sorrow over his dead dog, the overly confident Bonhoeffer sits in fear and trembling.

It is next to the ten-year-old that Bonhoeffer is pulled beyond theology and into the theological, beyond the academic and into the ministerial. It is here, in youth ministry, that he bumps up against the possibility of the encounter with Jesus Christ through the concrete humanity of being this ten-year-old boy's place-sharer.

Bonhoeffer must give an answer, and a theological one at that; the boy will settle for nothing less. So Bonhoeffer connects the boy's love for Mr. Wolf and God's own being as love, explaining, in a way the boy can understand, how in God all forms of love are redeemed and taken into the very love of God. "So I will play with Mr. Wolf again," is the boy's response, embracing the possibility in joy.

But, now that the boy has had his suffering shared, leading him to ask his deepest theological questions – as he hears Bonhoeffer respond to him not with theology but with the theological – he cannot help but do the theological himself. He says to Bonhoeffer that he scolded Adam and Eve for bringing death into the world, for losing Mr. Wolf was an experience of a ruptured world that allows death to end love. The boy, too, takes a step toward the theological. Witnessing Bonhoeffer standing in the theological, so too the boy is drawn into the theological; watching someone do the theological, the boy does the theological himself.

This story is a shining example of what I mean by turning to the theological as opposed to theology. The theological is first the ministerial; it is the taking of the boy to your knee and sharing in his suffering, allowing him to narrate his experience. It is never beating the boy over the head with theology, but seeking to give responses that attend to the experience. It hopes not for assimilation of theology in the young person's brain, but for the wrestling with God in the questions swirling within the young person.

Bonhoeffer even reflects at the end of the letter on how surprising it was to see a boy, whom he imagined as only wild and excitable, come to such reflection. This is a boy who would resist theology, too active to listen or care. But next to his experience, in sharing in his humanity, Bonhoeffer enters with him into the theological, igniting his imagination, seeing him transformed from a wild, uninterested boy to one who wrestles with God next to his deepest questions of lost love.

The death of Mr. Wolf forced Bonhoeffer to be nimble, to be a true theological thinker. In our day, so many in our own churches think they want a children's or youth minister who can teach their kids theology, believing that if the leader knows theology their kids will be safe, good, and informed enough to never ask their parents or other adults the theological questions that inevitably make them feel – like Bonhoeffer – small and unsure in the thin air of inquisition. But in this very thin air of the theological, the transformational occurs; it is where weeping turns to laughter, as Bonhoeffer says at the end of his letter. Bonhoeffer helps us see that a minister of youth and children is not someone who heaves theology onto young people, getting them to know stuff, but is rather a minister of the gospel who stands near the concrete humanity of young people, sharing in their experience, helping them wrestle with God's action in and through their concrete lives. *That is the theological!*

I wish I had been brave enough to say to the kind person that day, "Why do you think kids need theology?" Having genuinely listened, I imagine I might have responded, "Well, I'm not sure kids need *theology*; I'm not sure they need better curriculum or youthful versions of Paul Tillich, or even youth pastors that know every answer of theology. But what I do think they need is for our youth ministries to create open spaces with mission trips, retreats, and confirmation classes where young people's questions can be asked; where adults and kids together might narrate their experience of dead dogs, divorced parents, and rejection from their dream school and dreamy boyfriends. Ministering to them in these experiences we might await something more than theology; we might await the theological, that place where thinking about God and doing ministry come together."

---

[1] This chapter originally appeared in the November/December 2014 issue of *Youthworker Journal*, with the title "Why Theology Isn't Enough for Youth Ministry: Bonhoeffer, Dead Dogs and a 10-Year-Old's Tears." It has been edited for inclusion in this book.

[2] Dietrich Bonhoeffer, *Barcelona, Berlin, New York: 1928–1931* (Minneapolis: Fortress, 2008), 138.

Chapter 4

Christian Constructions of Children and Youth: Gift, Task, and Agent

Bonnie J. Miller-McLemore

In a congregation we attended while our kids were growing up, the teens had slowly gravitated over the years from sitting with their families to a pew of their own[1] and on one particular morning, when the youth minister was preaching several years ago, more than the usual number of teens were sitting together in the left front rows. Since my own sons were among the drifters, preferring to sit next to their friends rather than by me (imagine that!), I knew how much these kids admired and loved their minister and how well she knew and loved them.

Yet when she delved into the text for the day, she spoke right past the people she knew best. She didn't turn toward them or mention their hardships or joys. In fact, neither her words nor her physical posture gave any indication that she had a close relationship with them. Although not her intention at all – indeed, in

Bonnie J. Miller-McLemore is E. Rhodes and Leona B. Carpenter Professor of Religion, Psychology, and Culture at the Divinity School and Graduate Department of Religion of Vanderbilt University. She is author, co-author, and editor of over 12 books, including *The Wiley-Blackwell Companion to Practical Theology, Children and Childhood in American Religions, In the Midst of Chaos,* and *Let the Children Come.*

contrast to her great ministry with the kids – she essentially rendered them invisible, which is what many of us do in congregations, whether by ignoring kids *or* by including them in cute and token ways. At the time, I remember wishing that she had done something truly revolutionary and had spoken only to the kids, ignoring the adults completely.

I might not have noticed this dynamic if I hadn't birthed and raised three boys (now in their 20s) and devoted hours of research and teaching to the study of women and children as groups silenced, ignored, misunderstood, and stereotyped.[2] People tend to idealize *and* devalue women and kids *all at the same time*. My mission, then and now, is to render kids visible, as fully human people with needs for protection and greater integration in religious communities. For, while the church has stood quietly by, the wider culture has happily filled in today's picture of who kids are and what they need. In this chapter I want to examine five problematic portraits that thrive in the wider culture (kids as innocent, commodity, consumer, burden, and expendable) and three contrasting ways we might re-imagine kids from a revitalized Christian perspective (kids as gift, task, and agent).

Damaging Images

Even the idea that cultural images of kids evolve over time and place is a new and important insight. Art historian Anne Higonnet brought this message home for me. Her book *Pictures of Innocence* provides a vivid portrait of how Western society's view of kids has evolved, from pre-modern images of adult-like children, to what she calls the "Romantic child" in the last few centuries, to today's "Knowing child" who blurs the sharp distinction between adult and child. She contrasts colonial representations in which European children of the upper class wear grown-up fashions and adopt regal stances, hands on hips and one leg extended, designed to indicate their future adult status, with 18th-century portraits of the endearing, soft image of the naturally Innocent child. This Romantic child, which endows European children with an almost celestial goodness, pure and unsullied by worldly corruption, innocent, and even sacralized, "simply did not exist before the modern era," according to Higonnet.[3]

Although Higonnet thinks the era of the Romantic child has passed, I'm less sure. The problem with the Western construction of innocence is that it has led adults to see children as cute, but less often as capable, intelligent, or desiring individuals in their own right. The notion of innocence allows us to picture kids as passive, trivial, and even available to adult objectification and abuse. Equally problematic, the Romantic child defines children in terms of what adults are not – in Higonnet's words, "not sexual, not vicious, not ugly, not conscious, not damaged."[4] Such absolute distinctions between adult and child ignore the complexities of childhood, and they particularly strand adolescents, as if they should metamorphose overnight from child to adult and spare us the difficulties of their ambiguous in-between status.

Three other damaging images grow out of the economic sphere – kids as commodities, consumers, and burdens, or what ethicist Todd Whitmore describes as the threefold "anthropology" of unrestrained capitalism. As *commodities*, kids are used as a means to some other end. Whitmore sees this as especially prevalent in new reproductive technologies, where children become an "'investment' from which the parents expect a 'return' in the form of a 'quality' child."[5] I also see this operating in mundane family life. While writing *Let the Children Come*, I became especially troubled by what I describe there as a "middle-class obsession with securing one's own children's success with hardly a thought for other children, and paired with this, the extent to which parents use their children's accomplishments in soccer or math or violin to somehow feel better about themselves."[6] Modern psychology has described how narcissistically needy parents use kids as a means to meet their own desires for achievement and self-assurance. A child must excel in school or competitive sports because the parent needs the emotional gratification and affirmation.[7]

Capitalism also defines children's value around what they *consume*. The U.S. corporate world has turned kids into a new "retailer's dream." It has even coined the term "Tweens" for a group of consumers between ages 8 and 14 that comprises a multi-billion dollar market. Businesses have created an entire consumptive world of products around children, driven largely by television advertising, where shows and movies are coupled with products or the program itself is the commercial.[8]

A troubling casualty in this capitalist anthropology is the construction of kids as *burden*. Those unable to produce or consume have no real place in a market anthropology and can easily be perceived as little more than a burden. A good example of this perception appears in the lore about the costs of raising children. Estimates of the expense make regular headline news. Several years ago when I first studied cultural constructions of children, an editorial cartoon in the daily news appeared, showing two parents holding a newspaper with the headline: "Cost of Children $233,530." They look at their slouching teenager, then back at each other, and remark, "Seems our investment's taken a downturn." Such public pricing of kids as a major family liability is relatively new. But an economic schema that reduces everything to cash value has a fundamental flaw in relationship to kids. It creates a two-tier division between "those who have the wherewithal to produce and consume and those who do not."[9]

Immature and outside the economy, kids are especially vulnerable. Unable to produce or consume, they ultimately become a burden.

Finally, one further aberration of a Western anthropology that follows the perception of kids as a burden is the view of kids as *expendable*. An attitude and politics of benign neglect and outright disregard is especially apparent among those in the dominant culture toward kids in non-dominant communities and contexts. As seen more recently along the U.S. southern border and on the streets of Ferguson in the summer of 2014, kids are often perceived as acceptable collateral damage of racial, economic, and political conflict. Nearly 40,000 kids – mostly teens but some as young as five – crossed the U.S. border in 2013 seeking refuge from Mexico, Guatemala, Honduras, and El Salvador, and the number was expected to double in 2014. These children seek help for impoverished families, they flee family and social violence, and they pursue family members in the United States. And yet, because they are housed in guarded temporary facilities and caught up in strident government partisanship around immigration, they often become invisible casualties of poverty and unrest. Likewise, the crisis in Ferguson, where an unarmed teen named Michael Brown was shot dead by a police officer, powerfully reflects how the lives of young people who are already economically and socially vulnerable become even more precarious in a society that cannot assure their safety and survival, or offer a better future. Yet all too often their needs and hopes get lost in political name calling and power plays that ignore deeper problems surrounding our distorted perceptions of teens and children as expendable.

Countervailing Understandings

What "countervailing understanding[s]" does Christianity have to offer?[10] Unfortunately, Hallmark has trivialized one primary conviction at the heart of both the Jewish and Christian traditions that has great meaning and importance – kids as gift. For Christians, calling kids *gift* does not mean waxing starry-eyed and dreamy about them, as we've been misled to believe. This rose-coloured lens has even tainted how we read passages in which Jesus welcomes children in the synoptic gospels. We have wrongly associated receiving "as a little child" with qualities such as purity, humility, trust, simplicity, and receptivity. Certainly, both Matthew and Luke refer to "humbling oneself."[11] But the Greek word "to humble" has itself been misread as an entirely *emotional* and *sentimental* term, similar to meekness or modesty, rather than as a *political* and *economic* term, referring to powerlessness or social insignificance. Power and significance is precisely what children lacked in the Greco-Roman world. They were almost entirely at the mercy of the head of the household. The free adult male Roman citizen set the standard. By comparison, children were seen as deficient, immature, and irrational. The notion that children might be equal persons in God's sight was foreign. Indeed, they were, in the words of biblical scholar Judith Gundry-Volf, the "least-valued members of society."[12]

So the imperative to receive the kingdom "like a child" in Mark 10 must be read in light of the imperative in Mark 9:33–37 to receive children, literally – in their inferior and vulnerable social status in the first-century Greco-Roman world.[13] Children represent another instance in which a group, like women and the poor, is marginalized and dominated by more powerful people. They are models of discipleship precisely from this position, as the "least" in the family and society. Jesus *intercedes* on their behalf, *and* he *grants* them almost divine status. He is not just using children as exemplars, however. He asks his followers, literally, to attend to children. In the "demonstrative action"[14] of taking children up in his arms, he imitates a stereotypical female movement, according to Gundry-Volf, using the low-status activity of women's work as an example for his male disciples and thereby turning social hierarchies completely upside down. He "thus redefines care for children as a mark of greatness."[15]

Of course, Jesus didn't come up with this view out of thin air. Jews were distinct from the surrounding Greco-Roman world in recognizing children as an essential part of God's blessing, as is evident in stories such as Abraham and Sarah (Genesis 17:17, 18:10–15), and Hannah (1 Samuel 2:1–10). Jesus knew well the commandment, the *Shema*, at the very heart of Jewish law in Deuteronomy, to teach the love of God "to your children and your children's children" steadfastly, diligently – "when you are home and when you are away, when you lie down and when you rise" (Deuteronomy 6:2, 7). Kids represent not only the promise, sign, and guarantee of the covenant. They are participants in it, to be included in religious observances and routinely brought into the practices and beliefs of love of God and neighbour.

To call kids "gift" also means accepting responsibility to care for them as *task*, a second Christian reconstruction shaped especially by feminist theology.[16] If kids are gift, wholly unearned, they are ours "only in trust," as Whitmore asserts, coming from and ultimately returning to God. This limits adult power over them and forbids their use as a means to other ends. It also emboldens and requires us to care for them properly. It is high time Christians and our wider society recognized childcare for the labour it requires. Feminists have made us well aware of this. They have legitimately demanded that fathers and society bear more of the economic and emotional responsibility. And they have called for a revaluing of this work. In so doing, feminists challenge modern idealizations of children as entirely malleable, and of nurture as something that women innately and easily perform. Long before my books on children, I urged parents and congregants to grapple with the necessity of sharing domestic responsibility in households and congregations more justly and fairly. Injustice in the mundane distribution of chores, like laundry, cooking, and cleaning, breeds wider injustice. That is, if a child's "first and formative example of adult interaction" is one of "unequal altruism and one-sided self-sacrifice," as political scientist Susan Moller Okin argues, then they learn early on not to expect justice between women and men in society at large. "It is within the family," in other words, that we have our first lesson in moral behaviour, according to Okin.[17]

Christianity has sometimes contributed to the problem by idealizing and foisting on mothers and women a kind of exaggerated self-denying, self-sacrificing "love" for children. At the same time, children need more caring labour than many people acknowledge. Only in industrial and urban society has the job gone to the mother alone, the "most unusual pattern of parenting in the world."[18] Even when other professionals, such as nannies, childcare workers, teachers, camp counsellors, and so forth, offer care, it often falls to the mother to ensure that these forms of child-rearing assistance are lined up. But in the course of human history, others within the wider social group have always assisted mothers – what anthropologists call *allocare*[19] – not because they are paid to do so, but because they are part of the community or "village," as Anne Wimberly reminds us in her chapter. Congregations are a primary place to foster such "other-mothering," a term in some African American communities for the crucial role of "fictive kin."[20] Christians have a mandate to model shared responsibility beyond biological lines. We testify to this at baptisms, baby dedications and, for some traditions, through serving as godparents or through adoption. We proclaim the church as a new family in Christ and our own shared adoption into the household of God. Such testimony represents more than merely ethereal wishes; we have pledged ourselves to material labour on behalf of kids within and beyond our own communities.

Finally, kids as *agent*: Anne Higonnet suggests that with the advent of what she calls the "Knowing child," we're in the midst of a major reconstruction of childhood on the "same order of magnitude" as that which occurred in the shift in the 18th century from the construction of children as sinful to their portrait as innocent. In place of the ideal of the Innocent child, "Knowing children" call into question children's "psychic and sexual innocence by attributing to them consciously active minds and bodies."[21] More than anything, the more realistic, less romanticized "Knowing child" presents a less simple alternative, mixing together sexual, moral, and spiritual attributes previously dichotomized. As Higonnet remarks, today's Knowing children are as much about "difficulty, trouble, and tension" as they are about "celebration, admiration, and passionate attachment." This confronts adults with "many more challenges as well as many more pleasures than any [Western] idea of childhood has done before."[22]

To include children and teens more fully as knowledgeable agents requires more time and patience on the part of adults than earlier models that assumed kids had little to contribute and that orchestrated decisions hierarchically, giving adults power and privilege. It requires the ability to attend closely to kids and to navigate wisely their multiple demands and needs. At the same time, children and teens are not fully developed and so not ready to assume full responsibility for their actions nor able to relinquish their need for care and guidance. Kids' greater sexual and moral awareness should never serve as an excuse for exploiting their bodies, or demanding they serve adult criminal sentences. So adults must orchestrate the fine line between holding them accountable and continuing to bear responsibility for their care and protection. In the end, adults stand to benefit immensely from a model of children and teens that recognizes more fully their gifts, knowledge, needs, and agency.

Walking the Line

How do we walk this fine line between recognizing kids as full participants in families and religious communities while still taking responsibility for their nurture and protection? Let me underscore the immense need *and* complexity of welcoming kids as agents by concluding with two stories.[23]

Several years ago, I accompanied one of my sons on an elementary school field trip to a 4-H agricultural centre. I listened as a woman explained the processes of dairy production on a farm in bygone years to two classrooms of third-grade children. She displayed an antique butter-churn and several other implements used to get butter from cow to table. Who, she asked, did they think churned the butter? She was met by blank stares. So she hinted, "Do you have chores?" This was of no help. "No" was the resounding chorus from about 50 eight- to nine-year-olds. In the distribution of farm labour – not all that long ago, she made clear – children close to their age churned the butter.

That these contemporary children said no when asked if they had chores may seem like a small matter. But in actuality it represents a sea change in agency of major proportions, and about which we should all be concerned. Whereas today we often expect and demand very little of children and teens, not that long ago children had important responsibilities that contributed significantly to household economics. Kids need to see themselves as contributing to the welfare of the family by sharing in its labour. Likewise in the church, children need to have full access to the range of participatory actions of the church – acts of service to the community of which the church is part, the caring and nurturing of one another, and even the most vital decision-making processes of the church. Paradoxically, only by inviting them into greater involvement do we protect and nurture them in the long run.

The second story moves us forward a few years in my family life. As our three boys grew, we purchased a new round dinner table large enough to accommodate the five of us. Two of the chairs have arms. The others do not. One night during dinner, after the kids had traded places so the same odd-kid-out didn't always have to straddle a table leg, one of my sons noticed, "Hey, why do you two [meaning us adults] get the chairs with the arms [and leg space]?"

I can't capture the totality of our response, but it went well beyond chairs to a larger conversation about roles and relationships in which we tried to address the complexity of adult responsibility and kid agency. "We're the adults," we said, though this sounded a bit too much like the "because I said so" response. So we went on. "We are more responsible for your well-being now than you are for ours. We hope this changes eventually, gradually. We generally (although not always) have more experience, knowledge, and expertise." The chairs with arms are a small sign of temporary transitional privilege.

Yet the table itself is round. The heads of the table at which we parents sit are only marginally at the table's "head." "We are already trying to empower you in appropriate ways," we said. "We try to regard you with respect. We want your participation, as far as you're capable, in decisions that affect your bodies and minds."

Even in such small ways – how we sit at table with our kids, how we talk with them, how we distribute household chores and church duties – I invite us all to welcome children as *gift*, to share justly the *task* of their care, and to grant them *agency* through a gradual, incremental transfer of power and responsibility appropriate to their capacities. Religious communities that have long held up children as essential and important participants in religious life have a crucial role to play in countering negative cultural images of kids as innocent, commodity, consumer, burden, and expendable, and in offering richer understandings ground-ed in long-standing traditions, scriptures, rituals, and everyday practices.

---

[1] I'm thinking here of Virginia Woolf's *A Room of One's Own.*

[2] Because I was asked to talk about Christian constructions of children and teens, my presentation at the 2014 Faith Forward gathering drew upon previous publications where I develop more fully the ideas that appear in this chapter. For a more detailed examination of the content in this chapter, see my books *Also a Mother: Work and Family as Theological Dilemma* (Nashville: Abingdon, 1994); *Let the Children Come: Reimagining Childhood from a Christian Perspective* (San Francisco: Jossey-Bass, 2003); and *In the Midst of Chaos: Care of Children as Spiritual Practice* (San Francisco: Jossey-Bass, 2006).

[3] Anne Higonnet, *Pictures of Innocence: The History and Crisis of Ideal Childhood* (New York: Thames and Hudson, 1998), 15.

[4] Ibid, 224.

[5] Todd David Whitmore with Tobias Winright, "Children: An Undeveloped Theme in Catholic Teaching," in *The Challenge of Global Stewardship: Roman Catholic Response*, edited by Maura A. Ryan and Todd David Whitmore (Notre Dame: University of Notre Dame Press, 1997), 171.

[6] Bonnie J. Miller-McLemore, *Let the Children Come*, xxi. See, in particular, Alice Miller, *The Drama of the Gifted Child*, trans. Ruth Ward (New York: Basic Books, 1981, 1986).

[7] Ibid., 31–32.

[8] For further exploration of the impact of consumerism on children, see Mary Doyle Roche, *Children, Consumerism, and the Common Good* (Lanham, MD: Lexington, 2009) and Joyce Ann Mercer, *Welcoming Children: A Practical Theology of Childhood* (St. Louis: Chalice, 2005).

[9] Whitmore with Winright, "Children: An Undeveloped Theme," 170–171.

[10] Ibid., 175.

[11] For example, Matthew 18:4, Luke 18:14.

[12] Judith Gundry-Volf, "Between Text and Sermon: Mark 9:33-37," *Interpretation* 53, no. 1 (1999): 58.

[13] James L. Bailey, "Experiencing the Kingdom as a Little Child: A Rereading of Mark 10:13-16," *Word & World* 15 (1995): 59. Bailey relies on Ched Myers, *Binding the Strong Man: A Political Reading of Mark's Story of Jesus* (Maryknoll, NY: Orbis, 1988), 266–271.

[14] See Vernon K. Robbins, "Pronouncement Stories and Jesus' Blessing of the Children: A Rhetorical Approach," *Semeia* 29 (1983): 62–70, cited by Bailey, "Experiencing the Kingdom," 60.

[15] Judith Gundry-Volf, "The Least and the Greatest: Children in the New Testament," in *The Child in Christian Thought*, edited by Marcia Bunge (Grand Rapids: Eerdmans, 2001), 43.

[16] I build here on Bailey's interpretation of Mark. He argues that Jesus' action of taking up the children "embodies the dynamic of God's kingdom: welcoming and blessing the children epitomizes God's gracious reception of the vulnerable and needy. In summary, then, this story offers readers the kingdom of God both as gift and task." It bestows blessing and invites "responsible action on our part" (Bailey, "Experiencing the Kingdom," 62).

[17] Susan Moller Okin, *Justice, Gender, and the Family* (New York: Basic Books, 1989), 14, 22.

[18] Elizabeth Janeway, *Cross Sections: From a Decade of Change* (New York: William Morrow, 1982), cited by bell hooks, *Feminist Theory: From Margin to Center* (Boston: South End, 1984), 143.

[19] See, for example, Sarah Blaffer Hrdy, *Mother Nature: A History of Mothers, Infants, and Natural Selection* (New York: Pantheon, 2000); Sarah Blaffer Hrdy, *Mothers and Others: The Evolutionary Origins of Mutual Understanding* (Cambridge: Harvard University Press, 2011); Melvin Konner, *The Evolution of Childhood: Relationships, Emotion, and Mind* (Cambridge: Harvard University Press, 2010).

[20] Patricia Hill Collins, *Black Feminist Thought: Knowledge, Consciousness, and the Politics of Empowerment* (New York: Routledge, 1991), 119–120.

[21] Higonnet, *Pictures of Innocence*, 12.

[22] Ibid., 224, 209.

[23] Both stories appear in my books *Let the Children Come*, 2; and *In the Midst of Chaos*, 60–61, 89–90.

Chapter 5

Faith vs. Doubt vs. Wonder: How I Fell through the Floor

Kevin Alton

Everything I have ever experienced in faith and ministry is best expressed in terms of "journey." I've never been able to get my head around any sense of having *arrived* in either of those two aspects of my life and the idea itself just doesn't make any sense to me. Ministry changes by the minute and faith can change by the thought. There's hardly any ground called "here" to be had. Where we are is only on the way from where we were to where we might be.

But I've always wanted to "have" faith. I wanted to get it, to put faith in my pocket, where I could readily produce it when necessary for display or recollection. I didn't realize as a kid, and have only recently been able to express, the difference between *faith* and a *belief system*. As a youth worker, there have been times

Kevin Alton (kevinalton.com, @elvisfreakshow) is an author and speaker on all things spiritual and related to age-level Christian ministry. He is executive editor for The United Methodist Reporter website, senior writer and editor for the Youthworker Movement website, and co-creator of the Wesleyan curriculum website Youthworker Circuit. Kevin lives in the Georgia woods just outside of Chattanooga, Tennessee, with his wife Britta and their two boys, Grey and Penner.

when I've felt stretched a little thin by the personal spiritual transparency that's a natural part of youth ministry as a vocation. "Sorry kids, today Kev just doesn't have it in him to believe much of anything." Those kinds of days are a real and necessary part of any faith journey, but they're an awfully challenging place from which to lead.

But lead we must. So we walk in faith.

Faith

I am a Methodist. And ever so much more a Wesleyan. This is my tribe, my tradition, my belief system. It's the framework that I find gives me the best shot at recognizing and re-expressing God's love in this world.

I love my tribe, though there are places where we disagree deeply. There's a beautiful mechanism of faith expression lifted from the theology of John Wesley that gives voice to the sources that inspire and guide our journey. We call it – bear in mind that Methodists generally are a bit tedious when it comes to naming things – the quadrilateral. It's composed in equal parts of scripture, tradition, reason, and experience, with scripture being slightly more equal than the rest. What I love about the quadrilateral is the ability for its voices to speak in tension. Think of four friends in good-hearted conversation; they may disagree or even contradict each other at times, but great truth can usually be found in their overlapping agreements. None of the four is allowed to trump the others without regard. It just sounds healthy, doesn't it?

I've used the quadrilateral extensively in the way I teach and lead as a youth worker (though I doubt many of my kids realize it) and I'll use it here again; I see similar structure and conversation in the ministry practices of other denominations and faith traditions. As I've continued in ministry and my own journey through faith, doubt, and wonder, I've become increasingly bothered that we've let some of our practices and understandings of scripture, tradition, reason, and experience grow a little thin – or at least poorly defined.

Scripture

In my lifetime I have spent perhaps an abnormal amount of time in scripture. As a kid, I was fascinated with it, particularly with all of the sex and violence. My interest grew more normative through my time as a youth and on into college through an education that twisted and turned its way into becoming a B.S. in Ministry Studies (arguably one of the more honestly named degrees). The profession of full-time youth ministry submerged me in scripture, and I was further baptized by building a side career writing for various children's and youth ministry publishers.

In all of that time spent wading, gleaning, studying, and exegeting, I began to realize something odd – *we Christians don't always seem to have or even want a lot of knowledge about scripture.*

Much of our typical interaction with scripture is incidental to some other cause, like daily inspirational "somethings," or can I date/be/hire a divorced person, or, more to the point, how and when do I get to go to heaven and who else might I find there. We prefer, if we must read it at all, for it to be interpreted through sermons, conferences, or YouTube videos for today's culture, or through modernized language in fan-fiction like *The Message* (I'm kidding; don't get your paraphrase in a wad).

The problem that I see kids (and adults) run into – especially when their approach to scripture involves self-centred preconceptions about *what it is for* and *what they need from it* – is that instantly this incredible source of a history of humanity's understanding of God is being asked very narrow questions by me, *for* me, several millennia and a handful of languages later. Both the literal and historical contexts are often left behind (no pun intended).

I recently worked on a project for a new NRSV Bible that required me to read through most of the Old Testament. I had to *really* read it – not just stick with the familiar bits. I can remember at one point realizing that my mouth was just hanging open, slack-jawed in disbelief at how *supremely jacked up* some of those stories are. The next Sunday, I read Genesis 19 to my high school Sunday school class. At some point during the chapter, I stopped and said, "Can we agree that if I was reading this from *anything* other than the Bible I would be *fired* right now?" I couldn't decide which would bother me more – if Genesis 19 happened exactly as recorded, or if that's exactly how the writers of Genesis 19 *wanted it to be remembered.*

What we tend to do is to lift *comfortable narratives* from scripture, leaving the rest to be stored in the Bible like bonus content, B-roll unnecessary to the Oscar-winning plot.

But you're not supposed to do that with scripture, if it's Scripture. Some people have that angel on one shoulder/devil on the other shoulder thing going on. I've got a hyper-conservative angel-from-my-childhood on one shoulder and a… well, the other shoulder probably doesn't believe in angels. But the conservative one keeps yelling something about scripture being "God's Word." The teaching of my childhood and teenage years was steeped in the Absolute Rightness of Scripture on All Counts. If that is even fractionally true, you simply can't pull out one part over another. It's all or nothing. I'm not advocating for literalism. I'm arguing for a re-examination of scripture in its entirety as we interpret our faith around it, rather than trying to make it answer to our faith.

I am now not nearly as conservative as my childhood angel. But I wholly agree that if we're going to ask kids or youth (or anybody) to base any part of their faith on scripture, we're setting them up to fail (or just leave) by only engaging portions of it to paint a happy faith story. Young people see right through that crap. We're not letting them engage the differences between fact and truth – or, as Sandy Sasso says in her chapter, between what is *true* and what is *truth* – that open up the depths of scripture.

The urgent reality is that kids are growing up confusing their belief system with faith itself. Our belief system, of which scripture is a part, is simply the structure upon which faith can be built. When kids begin to poke holes in their belief system – a natural part of spiritual process – they fear that they're poking holes in their *faith*.

Doubt

I grew up – with my little shoulder angel – in a cloud of doubt. Because I was learning my faith in a church where faith was expressed primarily through the appearance of certainty, I spent an awful amount of time wondering why I wasn't so certain.

Reason

As an adult, I would eventually realize that a visit to the *dictionary* could probably have alleviated a lot of my worry about faith. The word *faith* is used broadly to describe the doctrines of the church. But when it gets personal, the definition is significantly less certain – faith is simply a strongly held position for which there is no proof. It's confidence and trust in something that ultimately can't be known, or at least not for sure. But as a kid, I was left to wrestle and worry, plenty.

As I grew older, I slowly came to accept myself and what felt like my own odd angle at pursuing faith. I found more strength in my connection to God in my *questions* than I did in my answers. I threw myself wholeheartedly into a pursuit of questioning God, scripture, salvation, miracles – whatever I could find to ask about. I became the youth volunteer that the kids knew could handle their "tough questions." Looking back, the sad part was that the kids were continually identifying as negative – their inclination to ask questions – what should have been recognized as a natural and healthy curiosity. They always were saying that they had "hard questions" or "real doubts" and often were afraid that God would punish them for using their brains to think.

What was complicating their ability to *reason* was what *faith* had become in their spiritual community. Faith had become an unquestionable "what *must* be true," instead of a living conversation about "what we *trust* to be true." It had become an odd mask of corporate agreement – "as long as we all agree that we believe *this* and nobody asks anything weird, we're cool. Now close your Bibles, don't re-open them, and don't forget to rewind the Beth Moore tape before returning it to the church library."

The culture of youth and children today is so globally connected that there's no room for that kind of neat, explain-it-once version of faith. This is true for adults as well, though we might be slower to realize or admit it. When was the last time you took a manufacturer's word when purchasing their product? Or a hotel's self-description when booking a vacation? We don't do that anymore. Knowledge has decentralized. I no longer need to go to Office Depot to talk to the business machines rep about computers. Partly because he no longer knows much about computers either – generally they stand there and read the information card to you, praying that you don't ask a question that isn't answered on it. But more because I don't even need to be in the store — there are far more answers *outside* of the store than in it. I ask the Internet; it tells me, with startling speed and accuracy, which is the best laptop for *me*. And it can usually be at my house before I could have made time to go to the store in the first place.

We simply can't ask kids to shut off how they engage culture when it comes to spiritual things. We're already at risk of losing them — clearly church is no longer viewed as an educational environment by kids. We've become the business machines rep, holding our card with the comfortable narrative, hoping no one asks anything that isn't on it. Unfortunately, our youth seem to self-select into two camps: those who are aggressively interested in anything and everything that *isn't* on the card, and those who aren't interested *at all* in what we're selling. When you can carry all of the world's knowledge in your pocket along with pictures of your cats and what you ate for lunch, you no longer *need* to know things; you *can*, in an instant, access anything you could wish to know. This carries over to faith in a strange way. Youth tend not to look to us for the *what* of our faith; that they can find on their phones, should they need it. What they may, however, be interested in is the *why* and the *how*.

Tradition

Churches that aren't intentional about engaging the honest struggles involved in a life of faith often end of up with pockets of kids wallowing in doubt. The way we choose to express our tradition can contribute heavily to the growth of this group. Kids growing up in an American expression of Christianity may be so steeped in the "we win" narrative that there's a natural presumption that our story is the *right* one and all others, therefore, must be *wrong* — even between the relatively similar pastures of Protestantism.

For example, during confirmation classes at a Georgia church where I recently served, something came up about store owners in another state hanging signs in their shops denying service to the LGBTQ community. Not wanting to stray too far from the intended topic, I tried to bring us back to point by simply saying, "That's a larger conversation for a different day. Whatever your opinion is on that subject, I'd encourage you to consider the strong crossover between the action of those businesses and similar actions by businesses that occurred before and during the civil rights movement." One kid shot back, "What does that have to do with us? We're not a business."

For a little perspective, the next week I returned with a church council record for our church from 1899. We read a few wonderful glimpses into the way people once used words (*"many a penitent throng gathered at the altar at the conclusion of services"* among others) and, after a few quotes, I showed them the cover of the ledger, which read, "Methodist Episcopal Church, South." You see, not so very long ago my tribe split over an argument about whether or not one should be allowed to keep slaves – which for many congregants was sadly more of a business concern than a moral one. The church I served came from the tradition that supported keeping them (hardly a point of pride or anything to put in the "about us" section of the church website). There our group sat, comfortable in its "we win" narrative, believing that we were Right About Things, ignorant of our own hurtful hand in history.

As my tribe once again faces difficult conversation about potentially dividing over how certain people are to be treated and/or welcomed as active participants in the kingdom of God, I think that how we've processed such a similar situation in the past should speak volumes (and at volume) into our current dialogue. Our kids may not be aware of the previous conflict, but they're aware of the present one and many are having a hard time reconciling the attitude of Jesus to the disenfranchised with how their church is treating them.

All of that, combined with an environment that seems to up-hold answers over questions, leaves out in the cold kids who have been taught to think and examine in every other environment. Their curiosities are now labelled "doubt" – which is totally fine as long as we recognize the value doubt has in a life of faith.

Wonder

I, as I said earlier, was one of those kids. For decades, I honed my ability to doubt. I asked more and better questions. If I couldn't ask them at church, I could ask them at the library or online. I dug deeper and deeper, wading into what could be a drowning pool of knowledge and argument about scripture, God, ecclesiology, grace, justification, salvation, eternity… and the proper pound weight of offering envelopes. It really is incredible how deeply one can go into a chosen spiritual rabbit hole and maintain the belief that this particular hole in no way connects to another.

For those same decades I encouraged youth to explore their own doubts, freeing them to ask questions they'd never felt safe asking, and giving them community, if briefly, to have those con-versations with others with similar inquisitiveness.

Then, with a collision-like suddenness, I hit a wall. With sharp abruptness, I lost my willingness to live into my doubt. I just didn't care anymore. The cause was simple: I woke up to the real-ization that even if I read every book written about God and faith, and watched every video made about Jesus and salvation, and heard every word spoken about scripture and kingdom and Spirit, *eventually,* holding full and complete knowledge of All Things Di-vine, I would on that day only stand at the brink of Mystery.

I was furious. I ranted and raged. I was sickened by all of the infighting, injustice, and presumptive hatred within Christianity that happens in the name of the holy, when, at the end of the day, we really know virtually *nothing* about God. What the hell are we fighting about? The crust of God? God's dust cover? Anything we know for *certain* about God is surely the least interesting part!

In the midst of my months-long tirade, I spoke with a long-time friend who has been at times an inspiration, a supporter, a collaborator, and, in this instance, a pastor. On the phone, pacing in my yard, I decried to him the suddenly irritating, meaningless pursuit of human knowledge. What point is there in pursuing a set of knowledge that, once complete, stops short of the heart of what we seek?

"It's like you're stuck in a library – just a room full of books," he said, "and you need to find a way to fall through the floor." It sounded brilliant, but I left the conversation with a "BUT HOW?" tattooed on the forehead of my faith experience. I wasn't sure if I could continue in ministry. I suddenly had the feeling that all I'd accomplished was to stand with my back to Mystery, waving my arms, insisting that kids (and I) define their faith within the books and available knowledge. Pay no attention to Mystery behind the curtain! After all, the books can assuage *some* doubt. But what does that really accomplish? If we resolve all doubt about what *can* be known about mystery, what have we really managed to grasp?

Experience
Months later, with the relief of a fever-breaking sweat, epiphany came.

As I once again stood screaming at Mystery about the futility of trying to know it, a thought occurred: *Yes. A Thing that Cannot Be Known. Isn't that incredible?*

I'd moved scarcely an inch from the spiritual geography of a moment ago, but where I'd been fighting to keep my head above the swells of doubt, I was now awash in the gentle rhythm of wonder. Let's go back to the dictionary (Merriam-Webster's, to be exact):

doubt 1a: fear b: suspect 2: to be in doubt about 3a: to lack confidence in; distrust b: to consider unlikely

wonder 1a: a cause of astonishment or admiration; marvel b: miracle 2: the quality of exciting amazed admiration 3: rapt attention or astonishment at something awesomely mysterious or new to one's experience

One experience is rooted in uncertainty and fear. The other is rooted in surprise mingled with admiration, caused by something inexplicable. Which of those sounds like God?

Wonder is everything we cannot know of God – hallelujah! When we begin to admit what we *don't* know, there we will finally and beautifully encounter the living God. It sounds a little charismatic, which probably makes even my angel a little nervous. But when we're willing to step into that which *cannot be explained*, we can begin to recognize the Spirit of God speaking all around us.

A final story from my life: My sons have discerning spirits. They can perceive elements of their surroundings that can't be absorbed by the five senses. They get it from my mom. She was seemingly able to know things that were absolutely unknowable about our lives as kids. It wasn't that mother's intuition garbage, either; her ability to perceive the hidden details of our lives transcended the need for physical presence, any parental snooping/ discovery process, and the occasional state line. I have that spirit too, but as a teenager I began stuffing it deep down inside in favour of cold intellect and reason (as an adult, I'm now working on letting it out). In any case, it's exciting to see that part of Mom come to life again in my children.

In the spring of 2014, the pastor of the United Methodist congregation that we were serving was moved to a new appointment. That's the way of the UMC, so it wasn't terribly surprising, but difficult news nonetheless as we'd shared life with him and his family for all of our seven years at the church.

I arrived at church for work earlier than my wife each week, which meant that she was stuck with getting the kids up, dressed, fed, and transported on her own. The morning of our pastor's last Sunday arrived, and as it happened our household's preparation for departure went less peacefully than usual. With an understandably escalating irritability, Britta ordered and argued the boys through their morning routine and into the car – the kind of proceedings that eventually have a parent feeling on the defensive, regretting some of their words and unsure how to restore a loving atmosphere. As the dark cloud of the Alton family approached the door of the church, Penner, our youngest son, stopped, turned to Britta, and said these prophetic words: *"It's okay, Mom. I'm going to miss them, too."*

Behold, the Spirit of God. In tears, Britta realized that much of her morning's mood had been driven by mourning the loss of our friends. No way our son could have known that, apart from God.

For the longest time, I had thought of experience in our quadrilateral in the past tense, a reference to what our experience *has been*. But lately I've come to think of it as our experience of *this very moment* and all that will follow. Experience is our active conversation.

Experience is our ability (and duty) to inject ourselves into culture, not retreat from it, to stop coming up with a "Christian version" of everything and become Christian people *creating* culture rather than sub-culture. Our every word and deed as followers of Jesus should invite and engage the presence of God. Instead of trying to find ways to "add some God" to any given church program, embrace the idea that our collective presence brings God into the room. That kind of *experience* allows us to bathe in wonder, to finally engage the things we cannot understand about God. Our experience of God through each other helps erase the dichotomy between our spirit and God's.

So faith, at the end of the day, isn't opposed to doubt *or* to wonder at all. Those things, along with belief, are *integral* to faith. Faith isn't what we can fully express, as I had thought as a child and as young adult. Faith is the natural by-product of the internal dialogue between our belief system, our doubts about that system, and our awe and wonder that none of the above really scratch the surface of God. Ministry should definitely continue to develop the belief systems of young people, but we should stop offering it in a box labelled "faith." Belief gives us a common starting point for conversation, but the individual faith of our kids can become real when their belief is a *part* of their journey, not the definition of it. And with this faith in hand, they, too, can fall through the floor.

MeetUp

Story

Chapter 6

Dark Matter, Disenchantment, and Wile E. Coyote: Why Young People Need Better Sacred Myths

Melvin Bray

Taking a page out of Stephen Covey's playbook, let me begin with the end in mind. I make my living, in part, by telling stories. So it stands to reason that I am also invited to speak about storytelling, particularly the value of sacred myth. My goal in beating this particular drum, however, is not self-promotion; I'm not simply trying to get hearers to buy my stories. Nor is my goal for parents and grandparents, aunts and uncles, pastors and youth workers, neighbours and friends to better be able to ex-

Melvin Bray (melvinbray.com, @themelvinbray) is an Emmy award-winning storyteller, writer, educator, and social entrepreneur residing with his wife and three kids in the West End of Atlanta, Georgia. He's an active participant in multiple networks cultivating sustainable approaches to a life of faith, including Faith Forward and Atlanta Table to Action. He is co-editor (with David Csinos) of *Faith Forward*, and coordinating author of *The Stories in Which We Find Ourselves*. Melvin works to help communities of goodwill find better stories and scripts – ways of thinking and doing – in which to thrive.

plain our sacred myths, as if each story only means one particular set of things, and if we could just learn to explain those things more clearly, our kids would be all right. No, my goal is to compel everyone who cherishes the stories of our faith to *tell* better stories. Too often we leave the telling of our biblical narratives to the most strict and strident among us, or to those who oversimplify or systematize our sacred myths beyond usefulness. Then we wonder why these stories, which mean so much to us, don't resonate with our kids. For all those people for whom this registers as a tragedy, I want us to recognize our ability as individuals to do something about it.

Now please don't let my use of the word *myth* become an impediment. *Myth* is not synonymous with *lie*. In the study of literature, we learn that myths are those stories around which people-groups organize their lives. So when I speak of *sacred myths*, I'm speaking of how biblical stories operate in the lives of people of faith. They orient and ground us. They give us something to aspire to.

A Cartoon Genius

Let me begin with a trite, comedic tale and work my way toward the sacred. Those of us who grew up in the wake of the glory days of cartoons surely remember Wile E. Coyote in endless pursuit of the elusive Road Runner, a pursuit that never ended well for him. Every once in a while, Wile E. would even try to match wits with Bugs Bunny to the same disastrous ends. With Bugs, Wile E. would talk, conferring upon himself the title of "Super Genius." Even with all his positive thinking, no matter how hard he tried, Wile E. could never get something to eat. I used to feel so sorry for the guy. It was like the very laws of physics, odds, and a fair shake were all stacked against him. I mean, c'mon, even a blind squirrel finds a nut every once in a while, but not this guy. Try as he might, Bugs and Road Runner just seemed faster, trickier, and cleverer than he.

Dare I suggest that Wile E.'s problem wasn't a fundamental unfairness drawn into his two-dimensional world? It wasn't that the pencil gods were set against him. Neither did his inability to stop his stomach from growling have anything to do with either Road Runner or Bugs outsmarting him. His hunger pains echoed his own failures of imagination.

"Failures of imagination?" you and Wile E. howl in response. And, like my wife, you begin to tick off all the elaborate schemes and contraptions Wile E. designed, built, or bought in pursuit of that one bite that would make it all worthwhile. While he certainly had some imagination, it was obviously not the imagination he needed, for no matter how creative he was in pursuit of his prey, the limits of his ingenuity left him unfulfilled. Meanwhile, Bugs was always munching on his signature fetish and Road Runner had to be eating something, because one just can't run that fast for that long on an empty stomach.

In his memoir, Chuck Jones, creator of Wile E. Coyote, divulged a list of rules that he lived by in directing the majority of the Road Runner and Wile E. cartoons. Rule #3 reads, "The Coyote could stop anytime."[1] But he doesn't. He never even seriously considers it. For more than 60 years, Wile E. persists in single-minded determination, not toward satisfying his need for food, but toward the one or two interpretations of satisfaction upon which he has fixated. Wile E. is the quintessential fanatic: "one who redoubles his effort when he has forgotten his aim."[2]

Wile E. could have simply walked away, recognizing there were slower and less "wascally" (to quote fellow Looney Tooner Elmer Fudd) dinner options for him, even in the American southwestern desert. He could have evolved, as it were (like the sharks in *Finding Nemo*[3]), making dietary concessions that put him in league with Road Runner and Bugs, not in opposition to them. Had he ceased to be a threat, perhaps Mr. Coyote could have established some sort of symbiotic collaboration with them to lure some other prey into one of his traps. But he does none of these things. He allows his view of himself as "genius" – like we Christians view ourselves as faithful – to restrict him to only three alternatives: catch the bird, catch the rabbit, or starve.

There are plenty of people who would tell us that this type of narrowing of scope, this singularity of purpose, is requisite to success. Just google "wile e coyote business" and you will see what I mean. And for many of us, this is how we go about ministry with children and youth. Too often we define our goals narrowly: the kids will be able to give these right answers about this set of questions; our teens will exhibit these "Christian Correct" behaviours in these given circumstances; young people will derive these particular lessons from this set of stories "and apply them to their daily lives." If such myopia does not lead to success (i.e., more young people committed to the faith), it can only lead to disillusionment, both for us and for the young people we hope to disciple.

Now, disillusionment can be a good thing if it opens one's eyes to new options, but often it doesn't. It just makes one cynical, disenchanting young people's view of all that is possible and waiting to be discovered in the world, limiting them to only what is *not*. Cynics see what isn't, but are blind to what *can be*. If we don't want our kids to grow up cynical, we've got to give them better sacred myths – more beautiful, more just, more virtuous tellings of the biblical narrative – to enchant their way.

I know plenty of kids who have given up on religion, but they aren't actually atheists, though I've heard them claim that label to avoid further discussion. In fact, they are cynics. They could believe if they were ever to find something worth believing in. What they've given up on is the sorry, self-interested, self-serving caricatures of God and faith and faithfulness to which they were supposed to pledge fidelity come what may – no matter how nonsensical or unjust the demands of that commitment became. The psychic dissonance caused by trying to hold on to the so-called "right" way of thinking while everything around and with-in you is suggesting there are better ways of being in the world can in time wear you out. You become disenchanted. It's as if all the magic in the world has been sucked out of you.

Disenchantment comes in many forms, not just, "To hell with it." Oddly enough, many disenchanted people remain commit-ted to their myths exactly the way they've been passed down to them, long after those tellings of their faith stories begin to lose meaning for them. The most common examples of disenchant-ment I witness within the church are persons who may practise adherence to some of the core teachings of their traditions, but who check out at the most arbitrary junctures. We've all seen it: folks looking for "fire insurance," so they put in their hour or two every weekend, but who live openly defiant to anything faith teaches any other day of the week. Or there are the anti–abortion faithful who aren't really "pro-life" – they're pro-birth, but once the child gets here they have no problem supporting "post-natal abortion"[4] in the form of war, untreated disease, food insecurity, economic exploitation, predatory incarceration, capital punish-ment, and the withholding of basic human dignities.

Disenchantment can also manifest in terms of folks like myself naming what we see as nonsense before having a name for what to do in its place. It's a pretty crappy thing to do to people: to suck all the magic out of their world with no plan for collaboratively casting a new spell. (Then we wonder why folks run back to the familiar and dig in even deeper.) By the way, this is why we desperately need poets, sculptors, painters, photographers, and storytellers to give us glimpses of more than just what is.

I don't mean to suggest that cynicism – which I am calling disenchantment – is limited to the narrow confines of faith traditions that fail to deliver on promises of a better world. It would appear that less religious inhabitants of late modernity are equally, if not more, spent on a world in which every attempt has been made to explain everything – leaving no more mystery or room for being proven absolutely wrong. Nowadays even highly respected scientists know there's more to life than what we can possibly understand. While not a religious man, Mario Livio, who runs the Hubble observatory, confesses that with everything science presumes to have figured out, some new mystery manifests – one of the biggest of which is this matter of dark matter, a reality we know little about but which seems to occupy more space than any other thing in the universe.[5] Livio's comments suggest that, even for the irreligious, a world divested of the magic of mystery (the expectation that there is always more to discover) is a pretty cartoonish world and, interestingly enough, other than the one in which we live. Such a world is itself a failure of imagination.

"Springs in the Desert"

If the problem of cynicism is a failure of imagination, then the challenge is to learn to imagine again. This process of re-imagining can open our eyes to meaning, to enchantment, in forms and experiences we may have long ago chosen to despise. It is a challenge that includes those of us who may have previously dismissed out of hand something simply because it was labelled "liberal," "conservative," "black," "white," "gay," "political," "anti-intellectual," "religious" or "of the devil" by someone else.

Re-imagining, as I use the term, is *affirmative critique* and *adaptive re-use* rooted in deep appreciation for the best intuitions of those who came before us. By *"affirmative"* I mean it's an attempt to improve upon, not reject, the past. I'm not sure one can re-imagine out of disdain.

Throughout my life, I have been faced with the challenge to re-imagine many times. It meant getting almost to the end of a degree in theology and deciding I needed to see if God could be bigger than my tradition. It meant having the LGBTQ kids at my first full-time teaching assignment befriend me long before I was open-and-affirming, and being loved by them before I knew how to love them in return. It meant getting in the car to go off to college as my fundamentalist stepfather took me aside and said, "If you're going to be a minister of the gospel you've got to be willing to minister to anyone and everyone." It even meant getting over my last little hang-ups regarding interracial dating when I heard comedian and activist Dick Gregory, then in his 60s, explain how he came to terms with his daughter dating a white boy once he realized he had given his life to creating the world in which young people judged one another "not by the color of their skin but by the content of their characters."[6] All of these moments involve ways of being in the world that I had to let go in order to imagine new possibilities. Where I am now isn't detached from my former self, but a re-imagined version thereof.

Re-imagining, as we are talking about throughout this book, is not the same as just making stuff up, finding our own way,

setting our own course. It starts with a common point of reference and expounds upon a shared sense of virtue. For Christians,
that common point of reference might be the virtues Paul names
as fruit of the Spirit – "love, joy, peace, patience, kindness, goodness, faithfulness, gentleness, and self-control" (Galatians 5:22-23,
CEB). Or it may be the radical challenge that Jesus issues in the
Sermon on the Mount: "You have heard that it was said, 'You
shall love your neighbor and hate your enemy.' But I say to you,
love your enemies, bless those who curse you, do good to those
who hate you, and pray for those who spitefully use you and
persecute you'" (Matthew 5:43-44, NKJV). Or it may be any of
the many other lists of cardinal virtues found in Judeo-Christian
scripture, like when Paul wrote to Philippi, "Whatever things *are*
true, whatever things *are* noble, whatever things *are* just, whatever things *are* pure, whatever things *are* lovely, whatever things
are of good report, if *there is* any virtue and if *there is* anything
praiseworthy – meditate on these things" (Philippians 4:8, NKJV).
These are Christian points of reference, common faith virtues.
Thus, I propose these virtues should be the starting point for re-
imagining the way we tell our sacred myths. If the way we tell the
stories from scripture fail to reflect these virtues – or reflects them
poorly – we need better tellings. And it is because re-imagining
is in this way embedded in a community and/or shared tradition
that it has credibility.

Many will wonder what right we have to execute a wholesale
re-imagining or re-interpretation of our stories. There are plenty
of justifications, including precedent. Our Jewish forebears had
ancient re-interpretive traditions, such as Midrash and Targum.
Within Christianity, although we don't always think of them as
such, each Christian denomination was, in effect, a new interpretive tradition that re-imagined the tradition from which it broke
away.

However, I find that the most compelling justification is when we ask, "What else can we do?" What else can we do when, for example, a myth as simple and as flawed as "enlightened self-interest" has so captivated the imagination of the Western world, overthrowing the ancient wisdom of most faith traditions and running our various ships of state so far aground, that we've forgotten the dream we had set sail to find?

Just think about the myth that says "people function out of their own self-interest." It is such a cynical worldview. And beyond that, our own experiences tell us it is simply not true. We've heard it over and over, to the point where it is difficult to imagine any other way of thinking about ourselves and about our neighbours. But rather than start by interpreting what we see before we even look, let's begin by just naming what we see.

Every day, firefighters as well as strangers rush into life-threatening situations to save lives. We hear poets serve up poetry seeking to inspire us, to give us tongues to taste more delicious possibilities – and they don't get paid for it. We see children in need of help, unable to find a parent, unable to tie a shoe, unable to manage their food, and we stop to help. We are people who function contrary to our own self-interest, day in and day out.

Thus, I submit that people do not operate according to their own self-interest; rather, they operate in ways that are deeply meaningful to them.[7] Sadly, the only meaning many of us have *is* our own self-interest. Sadder still, people of faith have not dared to tell more beautiful stories. We chime in with the story of self-interest as it is told by the cynics, never stopping to recognize how incongruous such thinking is with what our sacred myths really have to say about a life well lived.

"Used" or "Pre-owned"

Mythologist Joseph Campbell seemed to believe that re-imagining was one of the most important responsibilities of our time. He often suggested that if myths are to continue to fulfill their vital functions as time passes, they must continually evolve, because old mythologies that haven't evolved simply do not address the realities of contemporary life. It's like looking at a very old map of where you currently live. The map may not have on it your home or half the places you go on a regular basis. The map isn't "wrong" per se, but it is not very useful in terms of helping you orient yourself with familiar landmarks. Even if you were to recognize a landmark or two as you looked at the map, you'd have to constantly explain to yourself where that is in relation to other places you know. But, as Campbell has said, "A mythological image that has to be explained to the brain is not working."[8]

What we need in order to make mythological images from scripture work for the post-modern/post-colonial brain is not a mere updating of the imagery employed – which we often find in "contemporary churches" – but an acknowledgement of what we know better, what we've learned, since the image was first employed. All too often we try to use old images to justify or glamorize "the way things were," ignoring that the "good ol' days" weren't so good for everyone.

Take, for example, the traditional imagery of the subservience of women to men. "There's a hole in [that] bucket, Dear Liza." That bucket just doesn't hold water and it never did. Not to acknowledge this fact undermines one's credibility. To speak of "traditional family values" as those taught by the Bible minimizes the damage done in the name of those values and flies in the face of all the progress that's been made since. However, when we look back into the biblical narrative and begin to find all the stories in which traditional values were subverted in favour of a more sustainable way of being that enfranchised everyone regardless of gender, then the mythological image itself becomes more recognizable to our post-modern/post-colonial brains. And this gives our kids reason to be interested in what else the story may have to say. It's not that we have no use for stories that challenge our predispositions; we should just have no use for stories that set us back.

Boldly Going Where the Wisest Have Gone Before

We have had to give up a lot over the past couple thousand years, from thinking we and our earth were the centre of the universe, to thinking we and our earth were at least the centre of our solar system, to thinking our solar system was at the centre of our galaxy, to thinking our galaxy was the only thing like itself in the universe, to as recently as 1998 discovering that not only were we previously wrong about all of this, but the forms of matter and energy we thought we knew and had been exploring aren't even the dominant forms of energy in the universe. One would think that by now the only thing of which we'd be certain is that, at any moment, what we think we understand can be proven obsolete, incomplete, or flat-out wrong.

This logic notwithstanding, we are goaded through our politics, our religion, and the media into believing that changeability is evidence of some fundamental flaw. So we become tempted to try to hold on to our interpretations of the biblical narrative exactly the way they were given to us, even when those interpretations no longer make sense. However, if life is fundamentally changeable, then it stands to reason that we must be adaptable in order to continue to relate to it effectively. If we're playing tennis on a court that keeps shifting and we don't continually reorient ourselves to where the net has moved, pretty soon we'll be serving into the stands.

Even if we are not actually playing on a shifting field, we do know that our *understanding* of the field shifts over time. Thus, I would suggest that in re-imagining our faith stories, we need not seek a telling that has abiding credibility. We don't have to be right forever in the way we tell our stories. In fact, I would argue that, in light of the near certainty that whatever stories we begin to tell will, in time, prove themselves obsolete, incomplete, or wrong, our re-imagined faith stories should seek almost the opposite credibility. They should bear within themselves the seeds of their own deconstruction – that is to say they should be told as if they are not the one true interpretation. The credibility of *usefulness* within a specific context is sufficient, particularly if we are ready to admit that, at our very best, we are only doing the best we can with what we know at this moment.

The essential part – the part that makes this not an act of invention, but one of faithfulness, continuity, and improvisation – is that instead of mistaking our particular tellings of the myths for the virtues they help us imperfectly make sense of, we should insist that the stories we tell always reflect the virtues that gave rise to them. And when the imperfections of our stories become more pronounced than the beauty of the virtue they're supposed to teach us, we can give ourselves and others – especially our children – permission to let them go and re-imagine anew.

[1] Chuck Jones, *Chuck Amuck: The Life and Times of an Animated Cartoonist* (New York: Farrar, Straus, and Giroux, 1989), 225.

[2] George Santayana, *Life of Reason: Reason in Common Sense* (New York: Scribner's, 1905), 13.

[3] "Fish are friends, not food."

[4] I picked up this phrase from Don Golden at World Vision.

[5] In interview with Krista Tippett, *On Being*, NPR.

[6] From Martin Luther King, Jr.'s "I Have a Dream" speech (Lincoln Memorial, Washington, D. C., August 28, 1963).

[7] After first articulating this, I was introduced to the work of Harvard professor Marshall Ganz. Based upon this same observation, he has authored a whole theory of social action that provided the theoretical framework for the 2008 Obama presidential campaign. Learn more about Marshall Ganz's theories at http://marshallganz. com/.

[8] *The Hero's Journey*, directed by Janelle Balnicke and David Kennard (1987; Holoform Research Inc, Mythology Ltd. and William Free Productions), DVD.

Chapter 7

Tell Me a Story: Narrative and the Religious Imagination of Children

Sandy Eisenberg Sasso

I have been a rabbi for 40 years and I served one congregation for 36 of these years. Often during that time, religious school teachers have asked me what to do in the classroom when children ask about God.

I remember one third-grade teacher who came into my office, desperate for help. She handed me a list of 15 questions that the children in her class had been asking her: "Where does God live?" "What does God look like?" "What happens after I die?" and "How can God be everywhere at the same time?" The teacher asked, "Can you come into my classroom and answer all these questions?" I told her I'd be happy to come to her class – but I had no idea what I was going to do.

Rabbi **Sandy Eisenberg Sasso** (allaboutand.com) has served, along with her husband, as spiritual leader of Congregation Beth-El Zedeck in Indianapolis since 1977. In 2013, she became Rabbi Emerita and is Director of the Religious, Spirituality and the Arts Initiative at Butler University and Christian Theological Seminary. She is the author of several nationally acclaimed children's books, including *God's Paintbrush*, *In God's Name*, and *Anne Frank and the Remembering Tree*.

Then I realized that what I needed to do is tell a story. I related a narrative about a rich man and a poor man. The rich man believed God was eating the bread he had baked and had left at the synagogue. The poor man believed that God was giving him the bread he had found at the synagogue. When they learn otherwise, the two men decide to continue the exchange because, as the rabbi tells them, their hands (of baking and of receiving) are the hands of God.

When I reached the end of the story, I asked the third-graders to raise their hands. Pointing at each of their hands, I said, "Your hands and your hands are the hands of God." These children didn't need answers to all those questions. What they needed was a story.

Our Grandparents' Stories

In the 1930s, anthropologist Morris Olper recorded that among the Apache group of southern New Mexico, a person who had acted inappropriately would often be confronted and asked, "How could you do that? Didn't you have a grandfather to tell you stories?"

The educator Jerome Bruner suggests that it is not just the content of stories that is important, but the very structure of narrative. The way in which stories are constructed is the way in which we frame our experience. Bruner reminds us of how Peter Pan pleads with Wendy in Never Never Land to teach the Lost Boys to tell stories. "If they knew how to tell them, the Lost Boys might be able to grow up."[1] And this is exactly what we need to do. We need to give our children stories that they can grow with.

The first expression of religion is experience. We are people of faith because we had a religious experience. The closest we can get to that experience is story. Then the story is transformed into ritual and liturgy. Then comes reflection on the ritual – theology.

Theology is the furthest from the experience. The closest we can get is story. We want our children to get close.

Simple Language, Deep Concepts

James Madison once wrote that "Good books can put your mind and heart in a different place where the river runs deep. Good books can offer humility in our age of vanity, wisdom in an age of 140 characters."[2]

In much of what I have read in children's literature about God and about the meaning of life, I have seen an effort to simplify concepts, which assumes that children don't know how to engage these big questions. But when talking to our children about God, we do not need to simplify the concept. What we need to simplify is the language.

Craig Dykstra, former vice-president of Religion for Lilly Endowment, wrote that religious language must be "clear enough to be comprehended by young people, rich enough to be meaningful, concrete enough to relate to the world as it is, and critical enough to keep open the dynamics of inquiry and continuing conversation."[3] This, as it happens, is not just true for children – it is also true for adults.

When I write for children about the spiritual, I strive to create such stories, stories that use language in ways that are clear, filled with metaphor and symbolic images, concrete and personally relevant to children's experiences, and open to ongoing questions and conversation. I imagine that these kinds of narratives have the capacity to help our youth and children grow up. Whether or not they are literally true, good stories have the power to help us better understand who we are and what we believe.

But sometimes the theology we find in children's books does not match Dykstra's description. It may, in fact, be troublesome theology. Here is one story that I heard recently.

SANDY EISENBERG SASSO

The children were lined up in the cafeteria of a parochial school for lunch. At the head of the table was a large pile of apples, over which the teacher had written a sign that said, "Take only ONE. God is watching." Moving further along the lunch line, at the other end of the table was a large pile of warm chocolate chip cookies. And over this plate, a child had written a note: "Take all you want. God is watching the apples."

Sometimes the theology we give to our children is like this story. Our children need a deeper theology, one that can grow with them. At a recent family Passover Seder, I decided to tell the story of the Exodus in a Godly Play fashion. I spread out a long piece of felt and began to place wooden manipulatives as I related the events of the Exodus. There was a felt basket with a baby, a burning bush, Pharaoh, Moses, a few plagues, a sea, and a tambourine. My grandchildren's eyes were transfixed on these items. They were totally into the story.

After telling the story, I asked my family where they saw themselves in the story and who they might be in crossing the sea. Then I asked them if they had any questions. My six-year-old grandson looked at me and said, "Tell me, Bubbe: Is this story fiction or non-fiction?"

I wasn't quite ready for that question. But recently we had been discussing the meaning of the word *myth*. This six-year-old had explained to me that a myth is a story that isn't all factually true, but one that contains a very important message. So I answered his question by saying, "I think parts of these stories are like myth. I don't know if they all happened exactly the way in which they are described, but I know something big happened that was very important and has something to teach us." He said, "I thought so, because that part about the sea splitting couldn't have really happened."

My grandson understood that this was his story, a part of who he was. It gave him a sense of belonging to a community and a container to hold the abstract idea of freedom. And it allowed him an opportunity to grapple with the differences between what is *true* and what is *truth*. We talked about who we were in the story, about what we might have felt when it came time to cross the sea. In this way, we share one generation's story with another, and each new generation of listeners plays an interpretive role so that each young listener becomes a storyteller in her or his own right, a storyteller who appreciates the story – whether or not it "really happened."

Katherine Patterson, a well-known children's author, once wrote, "I did not want or need stories that told me to be good. What I wanted in a story was the same thing I longed for in a friend – I wanted understanding. I wanted to feel someone understood me. I wanted to understand myself. I wanted to make sense of a world that was frightening and chaotic. I didn't want a lecture, I wanted a story – a story that could make me laugh and cry and, when I had finished, would give me hope for myself and the world."[4]

Isn't this what we all hope for in the stories that we share with children? Because the truth is those stories never really finish; they continue in the lives of those who read them.

Reluctance to Talk about Spirituality

A 2008 Search Institute research study found that while a vast majority (93%) of teenagers believe that there is a spiritual dimension to life, only 14% said that their religious institution helps them in exploring their spirituality.[5] One in five said no one is interested in talking with them. But young people want to have conversations about spirituality. Unfortunately, very few of them actually feel as though anyone wants to talk to them about it.

Why is this? Some people may believe that children are too young, that they aren't able to have sophisticated, abstract conversations. Others may feel as though they don't know what to believe, so what could they possibly tell young people. Most of what we were told in childhood no longer makes sense. We assume that faith is about certainty – and we are far from certain. But in truth, faith is really about doubt. What Emmanuel Levinas said about the Hebrew Bible is also true for Judaism as a whole: "The language of the Old Testament is so suspicious of any rhetoric which never stammers that it has as its chief prophet a man 'slow of speech and of tongue.'"[6]

You do not have to be sure. Trust yourself. Noah was an amateur, and he built an ark. The engineers and workers who built the Titanic were experts. Don't wait for experts. What we believe will change over time. Don't assume because you no longer believe as you once did that you are no longer a person of faith. Faith isn't a destination, as Kevin Alton reminds us in his chapter; faith is a journey. And we need stories to accompany us.

Experiencing Stories

We who are people of faith have a large treasure of sacred stories, the places where our ancestors poured out their souls. We should not tell these stories just for instruction. We should relate them in ways that our youth can encounter them and find their place in the ancient narrative. But how shall we do this? How can we tell stories in our homes, faith communities, classrooms, and in any other place or time? When I share a story with children, I like to introduce it with a focus. For example, if I am telling a story that has to do with anger, I might ask, "Have any of you ever been

angry at someone? Can you tell me something about it?" Or if
the story is about fear, I might ask the children what it has felt
like for them to be afraid. And in this way, I begin with the child's
individual and personal experience.

Then I would say, "Now I'm going to tell you a story about
people who are angry" or "Let me tell you a story about someone who was afraid." And after I have told the story, I will ask the
children questions, but not questions that test them on how well
they were listening or how well they can recall the details of the
story. I don't really care whether or not children remember what
happened on the fifth day of creation. But I care about where
people are in the story. I care about questions that encourage
deeper conversation, not questions that test them on the facts.
Questions I like to ask are those that everyone can answer in very
different ways[7]:

I wonder what part of the story you liked the best?

I wonder what's the most important part of the story, to you?

I wonder what part of the story is about you and where you
are in the story?

I wonder what part of the story we can do without and still
have enough of the story?

These are questions that invite children into the narrative. They
are questions that help them see their place within the story.

Looking in God's Mirror

In my book *In God's Name*,[8] I tell a tale about people who call
God by different names. The farmer calls God *Creator of Life*. The
woman who nurses her newborn child calls God *Mother*. The
man who holds his baby's hand calls God *Father*. The little girl
who is lonely calls God *Friend*. The soldier who is tired of too

many wars calls God *Maker of Peace*. The people argue trying to decide which name for God is best, until finally they come together, look at one another in a reflective pool, and realize that all the names for God are good. And they call God *One*.

What we see in a story depends on who we are, our age, our experiences. No one face is better than another. They are all partial reflections of the one who includes us all.

It's a child's story – or so I had imagined. Before I read this book to children, I ask them to share their favourite name for God. Often they choose the names they have been taught by their parents or religious communities. Often they say *Father, Adonai, King, Hashem* – fairly traditional names. Then I read *In God's Name* and afterwards I once again ask them what their favourite name for God is. Very often, they will say *Mother* or *Friend*. I learned a great deal about God's name over the years of reading this narrative to people of all ages. And I learned the importance of giving people permission to name God based on their own experiences.

I read this story once at a Yom Kippur family service. A five-year-old child, one of a set of triplets, whose mother had been battling breast cancer since he was one year old, said, "My favourite name for God is *Healer*." The story allowed this child to name God from his place, to tell his story. It was the most sincere prayer I heard all during the long day of that fast.

I decided to try a similar exercise with adults, and I asked them to think about a name for God that best reflected the place where they were in their lives. I reminded them that there can be many names for God. After a period of silence, names came pouring forth.

One woman wanted to call God *An Old, Warm Bathrobe*. We all acknowledged and affirmed her naming – but I'll admit I thought it a little unusual. A year later, the same woman made a point of telling me how much that exercise meant to her. She told me that her mother had died that past year and she took her old warm bathrobe and wrapped it around her. It was then and there, wrapped safely in the robe, that she felt the presence of God.

I do not know God's name, but I think God must wrap around us like an old, warm bathrobe.

Stories have power not only when they are told and heard. Sometimes they can live dormant in our souls for many years, only to come alive again at the right moment. A young intelligence officer had recently returned home from a tour of duty in Iraq. He didn't talk much about the war. He was tired, glad to be home. To my surprise one day, I picked up the phone and he was on the other end. He said, "Do you remember that story you told about God's name?" "Yes," I answered, wondering why he decided to bring the book up now so many years later. He continued, "I now know my name for God. I want to call God *My Trampoline*. God is what allows me to bounce back after falling down." I do not know God's name, but I think God must feel like a young man flying.

Judaism teaches that God is like a mirror and everyone who looks into it sees a different face. What we will see in the mirror depends on who we are, our age, our life experiences, our emotions. No one face is better than another. They are all partial reflections of the one who includes us all. Stories can help us look in God's mirror.

But sometimes, instead of helping children name God in their own ways, we give children names for God. Often, children may not understand these names and the names may have nothing to do with their own life experiences. So they'll parrot back the names they know we approve of, the names we have given them to say. But in the process, they may stop looking in God's mirror and they may stop telling us what they see.

But God said, "Do not be confused if you hear many voices, know that I am one and the same. I will be what I will be. I will become what I will become. This is my name forever."[9]

The First Light of Creation

One of my most recent books, *Creation's First Light*,[10] is a story about the difference between the light of the first day of creation and the light of the sun and the moon created on the fourth day. It is a Midrash, a way of reading into the biblical text and filling in the blank space, those things that are not there.

Creation's First Light is a Midrash about the light on the first day of creation as a special light, a light with which we could see from one end of the world to another. It is a light that is perceived more through insight than eyesight. God hid this light after Adam and Eve ate the forbidden fruit in the Garden of Eden. But it was passed on in a jewel through the generations. In fact, it was the light that illuminated Noah's ark.

Some say that the light was lost forever. But I'll let you in on a secret: there are places you can find that light. It shines in the midst of a hug, through a giant smile, in a room full of questions, in a field of memories. If by chance you still can't find it, look into the eyes of a newborn baby and there you will see it shining as brightly as it did on the first day of creation. The light has a name – it is called a soul, the spirit. And we all have that light.

Birth may be a biological event, but it is so much more than this. It is a passing on of souls. A soul is not created out of nothing. It grows out of the hidden light of old souls, and you can see it in the face of each newborn child. When my children first became parents, I came to understand what creation's first light meant.

When you cradle a grandchild, you actually hold that sacred light in your arms.

Your great-grandparents carried that light within them. They passed it on to your grandparents. Your grandparents gave it to your parents. Then your parents took that light and passed it on to you while you were still waiting to be born. If you look deep inside yourself, you will find that light, because it is in all of us. And it is in our children. They can see it burning brightly, if we help them tell their stories.

1 Jerome Bruner, *The Culture of Education* (Cambridge, MA: Harvard University Press, 1996), 40.

2 James H. Madison. "Leade rs, Pundits and Reading Books," in *Indianapolis Business Journal*, August 31, 2013, http://www.ibj.com/articles/print/43226-madison-leaders-pundits-and-reading-books.

3 Craig Dykstra, *Growing in the Life of Faith: Education and Christian Practices*, 2nd ed. (Louisville, KY: Westminster John Knox, 2005), 125-126.

4 Katherine Paterson, *The Spying Heart: More Thoughts on Reading and Writing Books for Children* (New York: E. P. Dutton, 1989), 163.

5 Search Institute, *With Their Own Voices: A Global Exploration of How Today's Young People Experience and Think about Spiritual Development* (Minneapolis: Center for Spiritual Development in Childhood and Adolescence, 2008).

6 Emmanuel Levinas, "Revelation in the Jewish Tradition," in *The Levinas Reader*, ed. Sean Hand. (Oxford: Basil Blackwell, 1989), 197.

7 These questions are based on those often utilized in the Godly Play approach to religious education.

8 Sandy Eisenberg Sasso, *In God's Name* (Woodstock, VT: Jewish Lights, 1994).

9 Pesikta De-Rab Kahana 12:25.

10 Sandy Eisenberg Sasso, *Creation's First Light* (Indianapolis: IBJ Book Publishing, 2013).

Chapter 8

Foregoing the Zoo: What Fairy Tales Tell Us about Spiritual Formation

Danielle Shroyer

"Once upon a time…"

No matter our age, those four words beckon us to lean in to hear a story. Whether we are children tucked in bed awaiting the pages of our favourite book once again, young adults sneaking a book out of our backpacks during class to finish that suspenseful scene, or adults curled in front of a fire with a new novel, we long for stories to transport us, to inspire us, to enliven us. Stories form us, and, if we are lucky, transform us.

Fairy tales are some of our earliest learned stories and yet we

Danielle Shroyer (danielleshroyer.com, @DGShroyer) is an author, speaker, and blogger. An ordained minister, she served as the pastor of Journey Church, one of the first independent emerging churches in the United States, for over eight years and currently serves the congregation as an elder. She is the author of *The Boundary Breaking God: An Unfolding Story of Hope and Promise*, and the forthcoming *Where Jesus Prayed: Illuminating the Lord's Prayer in the Holy Land*. A graduate of Baylor University and Princeton Theological Seminary, Danielle speaks often across the United States on issues of theology, faith, church leadership, culture, and story.

do not soon outgrow them. In recent years in particular, there has been a cultural resurgence of fairy tales, from movies such as *Snow White and the Huntsman, Mirror Mirror,* and *Hansel and Gretel,* to popular television shows such as *Grimm* and *Once Upon A Time.* These well-known stories are being given updated, modern twists with an unapologetically adult flair, which reverses the trend in previous years to sanitize and animate these often gruesome tales.

This is, of course, what fairy tales have done for generations: they have been told and retold, tweaked and altered, lightened and darkened. Shared by women spinning around a fire-hearth, men travelling along a lonely dark road, and parents entertaining bored children, these stories have been carried by the winds of time across centuries and cultures. They are, it can be argued, humanity's common language. These tales beckon to that place within all of us that longs for adventure while staying safely at home. They invite us into strange lands we'd dare not travel, accompanying terrifying characters we'd be too frightened to meet but want to encounter nonetheless.

Fairy tales invite us into adventure, not just for the sake of adventure but in search of something. Let's not be fooled by the golden hair of Rapunzel or Cinderella's glass slipper: at their core, fairy tales are stories about finding meaning and purpose. They are adventure tales that lead us straight into the depths of our own souls. Fairy tales take us through unknown lands to give us hope that we, too, can arrive at a new understanding. It may not be "happily ever after," but it will be a place of transformation and change.

And herein lies a deep truth: the untamed nature of fairy tales is the very reason why the tales are able to tame us.

Is this not what we feel when we read certain stories from scripture? Despite thousands of years of translation and heavy-handed editing, our holy stories refuse to be silenced. They call us to sit with them, to struggle with them, even to find them baffling and unknowable. "Those who have ears to hear, let them hear," says Jesus. And often, we scratch our heads and wonder whether we can hear at all.

This is not a bad thing. In fact, it is a necessary thing, for it leads us into the heart of the stories themselves. The struggle to understand, to interpret, is the very process by which the Spirit often transforms us.

In recent years, as I have become rather enamoured with fairy tales, I have noticed time and again how their structure and function and intention run parallel to the process of spiritual formation. That is to say, fairy tales have endured in part because they create the same kind of environment that sacred stories do. Sadly, I fear that many of us who minister with youth and children have foregone this wild environment for more sanitized shores. We have too often prized indoctrination over imagination. We have tamed our lions and placed them in zoos. And we are surprised when visitors no longer find the lions as compelling or powerful as they were in the wild.

What if we were to set them free again?

If we want to undo the Bowdlerizing[1] influences of the past, how can we create an environment where we can once again experience the wild fullness of the biblical story?

I believe fairy tales can point us in the right direction. To show this, I'll share six points of intersection that I've noticed between fairy tales and spiritual formation that might help us re-imagine a way forward in faith.

Be Simple and Focused

One of the most helpful aspects of fairy tales is their simplicity, which may be an odd thing to say about stories that often make little to no sense to the modern reader. But simple they are, indeed. This doesn't mean they aren't *deep*. Even the simplest story can be engaged on a number of levels. What it *does* mean is that fairy tales have an intentionally limited scope. They zoom in on a very small cast of characters and keep the focus on a single plot line from beginning to end. There is no "offstage," no backstory or cultural milieu. There are no world wars going on in fairy tales. They rely on human experience rather than on cultural or national identity, which is what makes them so widely appealing. Fairy tales happen in an "anytown, anyplace" that is meant to be vague, and "once upon a time" is an invitation into a suspended space that is both everywhere and nowhere. Without extraneous details, fairy tales are both simple and timeless.

Characters in fairy tales are to be taken at face value. With very little description given to personality, appearance, and certainly motive, readers are forced to go along quite matter-of-factly. There is no build-up from one point to the next, no tension. The stories read more like a clap-clap-clap: this happened, then this happened, and then this. This uncluttered way of storytelling keeps the focus on what is most important – the character who is searching for something to change.

While that is indeed helpful, it also reveals why fairy tales are so compelling to children, who make meaning in the very same way. Children focus on the environment directly surrounding them. They tend not to ponder the world situation, or their actions in relation to the actions of someone in a different city, much less a different country. In the early years of formation, and then again in young adulthood, we are necessarily self-centred. Our own development, our own search for identity and self, takes rightful centre stage.

For adults living in an overcrowded, complex world, facing endless streams of information and input, the simplicity of the world of a fairy tale is equally attractive. Perhaps there is something necessary about setting down our geopolitical nuances every once in a while to read a story in which good and evil is so obviously pointed out.

The universal simplicity of fairy tales is indeed a central reason for their appeal. It makes me wonder why, as children's and youth ministry leaders, we feel such a need to cover the entire arc of scripture with our young people, or add in every moral but the kitchen sink when teaching them how to follow God. We may feel fine teaching two-year-olds just one simple idea, but by the time our children are in grade school, we may as well be preparing them for the Bible SATs. We add in object lessons and practical application stories and parallel passages of scripture and memory verses and take-home packets with ideas for the week.

What if we trusted the universal simplicity of a story from scripture? What if, at least sometimes, we allowed the story to sit by itself, and to teach us just what it does? If we can believe, with good evidence, that there's something about fairy tales that is enduring and transformative, which has allowed them to flourish for centuries, don't you think we should give at least that much credit to our sacred stories, which have endured for thousands of years? Can we trust that the stories, in and of themselves, may be enough? If a fairy tale told around a fire can reach people across hundreds of years, why do we doubt that telling a Bible story around a fire, just as it is, can do the same?

Leave Space

Fairy tales leave a lot of open space. Because of their skeletal structure, there is plenty of room to imagine. More importantly, there is plenty of room to imagine yourself in the story. We know so little about these fabled protagonists, but we follow them still. They are not meant to be analyzed. We willingly go into the woods with Little Red Riding Hood, and we stay with her every step of the way. In this way, we become part of the story. The story is not just heard, but experienced.

Many sacred stories, particularly those in the Hebrew scriptures and the parables of Jesus, are told with this same kind of open space and sparse detail. We're left with all kinds of questions. *How did the treasure get in the field? Who put it there? What did the man do to get the money to buy the field? When he opened the treasure, what was it?* These questions do not detract from the story; they go to the heart of the story itself. The experience, the wondering, is the very thing that changes us.

When encountering scripture, we also find open space. And yet, too often we are all too eager to fill it, uncomfortable as we can be with the unknown. Rather than feeling permission to "play in the gaps" and imagine, we worry about interpreting the wrong way, or misunderstanding the "meaning" of the passage. We do not trust that the space might hold a better answer than a flow chart proving the passage's logic. And after we've read the story, we do not always feel comfortable sitting with the questions that arise in its wake. We settle too often for answers, when the stories are intended to guide us toward *meaning.*

What if, instead of turning scripture's stories into Aesop's fables with a tidy moral at the end,[2] we allowed them to be more like fairy tales, with lots of open space that beckons questions and conversations?

Embrace the Strange

Fairy tales embrace the strange. They practically parade the strange in an endless procession – mice that talk, frogs that turn into princes, a girl the size of a flower, a kiss that brings a sleeping girl back to life. Fairy tales beckon us into a foreign reality that requires us to leave our rational intellect at the door for a moment. They ask us to look past what we know and into what could be lurking just underneath the surface. In this way, the strangeness creates its own kind of open space.

Fairy tales are intentionally, delightfully illogical. They force us to accept that a bird *is* talking, rather than ask whether or not a bird *can* talk. By using elements we know and putting them together in surprising ways, fairy tales ask us to imagine the impossible.

Faith, of course, does the very same thing. As Christians, we look out at a world filled with hatred and violence and anger, and we proclaim boldly that love is the strongest power in the universe. It may look illogical, but we believe it is the truth lurking just underneath the surface. We Christians are, if anything, a strange lot who follow a man some say is dead but whom we profess to be very much alive.

You would think we would be more comfortable embracing the strange, what with our scriptures being filled with stories of Elijah calling down fire from heaven, which lights up an altar soaked in water; Daniel surviving an entire night in a den of ravenous lions; Jonah being spit out of a big fish after three days; and Mary bearing a child that was foretold by an angel. Instead, sometimes we try to normalize scripture, to sanitize it down a bit, to make it more believable. In our haughtiness, we think ourselves too modern for such nonsensical tales, rather than trusting that these stories may in fact grow us up.

In the last 50 years in particular, we have used countless methods to make the Bible "relatable," from glitter-infused pink Bibles, to pictures of Jesus as a blue-eyed blond-haired model. We've made illustrated Bibles filled with people who look just like us, and added extra animals and clouds and sunshine rays so that it could very well be a Care Bears movie. And we've scrubbed the strange out of our places of worship, too, so that they could be rather easily retrofitted into a mall, or a big box store, or a movie theatre. But there is something undeniably strange about us, and there always will be. We speak of a different realm, and we follow a different servant King. What if, instead of being embarrassed about our strangeness, we embraced it? What if, like a good fairy tale, we paraded our strange in joyous procession?

Confront Evil

Fairy tales teach us about evil. They do so directly and without pulling any punches, which has made them rather repulsive to just about every modern parent who considers reading these stories to their children. And certainly, it would be unwise to share some fairy tales with a small child before bed. (Some seem to be worth forgetting altogether, like the story of the child who was always disobedient and was therefore buried in the backyard.) But what we ought to remember in a fairy tale's more sober moments is that they are brutally honest about the hardest truths of life. In a time when children died frequently and malnutrition was rampant, Hansel and Gretel is certainly morbid, but it's also an honest reflection of a child's worst nightmares – abandonment and starvation.

Fairy tales put words to some of our biggest fears, forcing us to confront them head-on. But they don't do so sloppily or without consideration. These stories expose children to the realities of evil in the safety of an imaginary nowhere. Children already know that evil is in the world, and they also know their parents don't want to talk about it. The tales tell them the truth they hear the adults whisper from the other room, and they do so with the added benefit of intrinsic safety, because the tales can tell them without actually making them confront it in reality.

As scary as evil in fairy tales might be, it is arguably the safest way for a child to learn about the shadow side of the world. And though fairy tales are not meant to be fables that teach a simple moral message at the end, they *do* communicate hard truths.

One of the most important of these truths is that evil is in the world and sometimes adults cannot be trusted to fight it, or to save children from it. Sometimes, adults are in fact the source of the evil. In tale after tale, a child is intentionally left alone. Red Riding Hood is far from her mother and did not reach the safe arms of her grandmother. Now that she's face to face with the Wolf, what will she do? Snow White's stepmother wants her dead, and her father is gone. How can she survive? Hansel and Gretel are abandoned in the forest. How are they going to make a way for themselves? In all of these tales, the characters are forced to grow up and become responsible for their own survival.

This is the goal of all parents: to foster their children toward self-sustaining maturity. In a culture filled with young adults who are often failing to launch, perhaps a few tales of survival would be good medicine. (And, perhaps, this is one of the reasons why young adults are so drawn to dystopian stories. Far from the reaches of helicopter parents, they are confronted with the primal need to survive under even the most dire circumstances.)

Our scriptures also speak plainly about evil. They expose the shadow side of our nature, and even of the practice of religion itself. Rather than running away from these stories, or worse,

editing them, perhaps we should consider the difficult yet necessary truths they communicate. David murdered Bathsheba's
husband, showing that even chosen kings can't always be trusted.
Even God's people are capable of killing and pillaging in the wake
of battle and victory. Even Peter reached for his sword and later
denied his saviour.

The shadow side of religion is already something children have
heard whispered from the other room. And if they haven't heard
it yet, they will. Rather than trying to protect them from it, why
don't we find the courage to engage it directly, and find a way
through it?

Remember that Evil Can Be Overcome

Fairy tales teach us about evil. But more importantly, they teach
us that we can overcome evil. They teach us that even if we make
terrible mistakes that land us in terrifying situations, we can find a
way forward. A girl marries the mysterious Bluebeard despite her
family's protests; but when she discovers that he is a murderer, she
finds a way to escape. Hansel and Gretel are at first duped by the
candy-covered house of a terrible witch, but in the end they find
a way to outsmart her. Fairy tales remind us that even our worst
decisions can be redeemed before it's too late. They call upon the
renewing force within us that gives us the power to overcome.

G. K. Chesterton said this best:

Fairy tales, then, are not responsible for producing in children fear, or any of the shapes of fear; fairy tales do not give
the child the idea of the evil or the ugly; that is in the child
already, because it is in the world already. Fairy tales do not
give the child his first idea of bogey. What fairy tales give
the child is his first clear idea of the possible defeat of bogey.
The baby has known the dragon intimately ever since he
had an imagination. What the fairy tale provides for him is
a St. George to kill the dragon.[3]

For our children to feel empowered in the face of evil, they need to know stories that show them it is possible to overcome it.

This is at the heart of the gospel message. In a world that is broken, God has called us to be people who repair the world, who mend the breach, who are in service of the Power that can overcome even death itself. God's Spirit equips us so that we can be "more than conquerors."

Our sacred stories tell us that evil is real. But they also tell us that evil can be overcome by good, and that Good will triumph in the end.

Experience Empathy

Finally, fairy tales teach us empathy. More precisely, these tales are a portal through which we can experience empathy. Because they are first-person, zoomed-in, immersive stories, children experience the full range of emotions that occur within a fairy tale. So children who hear "The Ugly Duckling" will feel the deep sadness and isolation of the duckling, the fear on the journey, and the elation of the duck's transformation into a swan. They do not watch the duckling as outsiders. For a short time, they become the duckling. In doing so, they experience depth by proxy; they may not have felt isolation to that degree before, but they have felt something close enough to it to empathize the rest of the distance.

Neuroscientists tell us that we develop empathy when we can imagine ourselves in another person's shoes.[4] Our neural pathways are opened up and strengthened when we practise seeing the world through the eyes of others. Because fairy tales are intended primarily to evoke feelings, they encourage empathy in very real ways. They provoke our sense of justice, our worries and fears, and our quest for transformation. They beckon us toward a happy ending.

For those of us seeking to raise compassionate young people, the empathic nature of fairy tales makes them a natural ally. At the heart of the fruit of the Spirit is deep empathy. For us to bear fruit, we must practise opening our hearts to others. Compassion and empathy are spiritual disciplines that are only fostered through repetition and practice. Stories that bring us into this deep knowing, this connected empathy, form us into the kind of responsive, generous, and kind people God intends.

How can we create an environment where we can experience the wild fullness of the biblical story?

In a world desperately searching for meaning and purpose, let us trust in the Lion. Let's stop caging the Lion, taming the roar, brushing its coat as we would for a house pet. Our Lion may seem simple at times, too prone to wandering the open land, too strange. But we trust that our Lion can confront evil courageously, and can overcome it. And we profess that our Lion knows our deepest longings, and meets us there with compassionate love.

Let's forego the zoo and walk with our children to the beautiful unknown wilds. If we do, we may just find our happily ever after.

---

[1] Named after Thomas Bowlder, who published a highly edited version of Shakespeare's plays to make them more amenable for children, to *Bowlderize* is to remove all the parts we find offensive, vulgar, or off-putting.

[2] Ivy Beckwith coined the phrase "Aesop's-Fableization" of the Bible in *Postmodern Children's Ministry*. She writes, "When we teach children the Bible simply to push forward a certain moral or theological agenda, we are guilty of what I call the "Aesop's-Fableization" of the Bible. Literary history gave us moral fables. We don't need the Bible to teach children moral lessons. We need the Bible to introduce children to God, God's story, and God's ways." Ivy Beckwith, *Postmodern Children's Ministry* (Grand Rapids: Zondervan, 2004), 126.

[3] G. K. Chesterton, *Tremendous Trifles* (London: Methuen & Co. 1909), 102.

[4] Christopher Bergland, "Can Reading a Fictional Story Make You More Empathetic?" *Psychology Today*, December 1, 2014, http://www.psychologytoday.com/blog/the-athletes-way/201412/can-reading-fictional-story-make-you-more-empathetic.

Chapter 9

All God's Children

Constance Bynum, Niya McCray,
and Romal Tune

In this chapter we encounter three spoken word poems, each introducing us to a different young person's story. These stories call us to question whether what we count as ministry meets young people at the point of their need.

Who's Looking for Me?

Romal Tune

We never went to church when I was growing up. But we did believe in God and we prayed that one day God would show up. Because it was going to take a miracle to change the things that we had to see. From drug addictions to drive-by shootings, to families living in their cars and teenage prostitution.

By the time I was in the eighth grade I got tired of asking strangers if they had change to spare and watching them cross the street or just look away like I wasn't even there.

Even a blind man could see that society didn't care about people like me. I guess they figured it was my fault for being born in poverty.

That's why most of my days were spent hustl'n on the streets so that I could at least buy some clothes and have something to eat.

Romal Tune (romaltune.com, @RomalTune) is the embodiment of living beyond the label. After overcoming the setbacks of his upbringing and the destructive choices of his youth, he is now a sought out communicator, community strategist, and education consultant. He is a graduate of Howard University and Duke University School of Divinity, an ordained minister, and the award-winning author of *God's Graffiti: Inspiring Stories for Teens.*

Because I remember the mornings when mother would wake me up for school, hand me three dollars and say I'm sorry but today you have to choose, between riding the bus to get home or using the money to buy some food.

It seemed like every day I prayed hoping that God would hear me so that my mother could stop drowning her sorrows in a bottle of Hennessy, always worrying about how she was going to take care of me.

We didn't have health insurance so mom couldn't see a doctor to deal with her depression; instead of medication she would open another bottle every time she started stress'n.

In those moments when I wondered if things were ever going to change, I just wanted somebody to tell me that you're going to be okay, that I know it's tough right now but there will be better days.

Because I remember sitting up with my cousin one night sharing a bag of chips and fantasizing about what our funerals would be like.

You know, things like who do you think will show up, who'll share stories and who will cry. Because it seemed like in order for people to finally see us we would probably have to die.

Imagine what it's like at the age of 15 to think that the only way to stop the rejection and receive some affection is for a pastor to close the casket and give your final benediction.

All I ever wanted was a chance to be free. For society to stop judging me with their stereotypes and personal insecurities. Because maybe then I'd have a shot at being unapologetically and authentically me.

Just like Jephthah in Judges 11, I found my place on the streets but all I really wanted was God to show up for me. The same way he showed up for Moses before he parted the Red Sea. And the same way he showed up for Joseph when he had a dream.

Because every time I closed my eyes and tried to dream of what the future holds, like Rahab all I had were the negative re-minders of things that I was told. Successful people don't look like you. You're not good enough because of what you've been through. And you don't go to church so why would God bless somebody like you?

How many kids are growing up just like me, or like Esther, Jephthah, Moses, and Joseph? Just wanting to be free and want-ing to pursue their dreams, hoping one day somebody is going to come looking for me, praying for people to open their eyes and see.

That I'm just like you. I may not have much but I have a pur-pose too. I may not go to church but God still loves me just as much as God loves you. In fact, God uses me because there's testimony in what I've been through.

I didn't go to church but I found sanctuary on the streets. And the people out here may not have degrees and prestige but they believed in me.

That's why I give God all the praise because everything changes. Faith got my mother off drugs and me off the streets, I served my country, then went to college and got two degrees. So now it's my obligation to the next generation by going back to the streets and help the people like me.

Now if that ain't God then I don't know what is. Maybe unlike some people God doesn't just help the good kids.

Instead of turning my back on people in the hood, it's my turn to give back because God had been too good. So for the people who are hurting and wondering if God hears you, Christians like me are answering the call and we're out looking for you.

See the church doesn't have the right to pick and choose who gets to be a Christian, because that's not God at all, it's just elitist religion.

That's why we can't covet Jesus and hold the gospel hostage in our church locations, because this is not about going to church. It's about the ministry of reconciliation.

And the kids on the block waiting on God to show up are hoping that we will tell the people who are trippin' on who's the better Christian, that it's time to grow up.

Because God doesn't make mistakes.

But people do. What you have been through does not define you. It merely proves that you are stronger than anything that has tried to stop you.

CONSTANCE BYNUM, NIYA MCCRAY, AND ROMAL TUNE

See that's what urban ministry is all about, telling hurting kids
that it's time to come out. Stop hiding in the shadows and
being ashamed of where you come from, but put your life in
God's hands and be the person you are destined to become.

(her)Story 101

Niya McCray

I remember when I first started school
I was one of those kids who got bullied for being too smart,
  never too cool
As my peers threw out hurtful epithets, to them I was the
  teacher's pet inside I became transparent
So apparent, you could see right through to the books, the pages
  that I hid in
Submerged my mind in tales of white whales, Call me Ahab, call
  me Ishmael
You could call me anything once I learned I was destined to win.
I was pleasantly plump, mama called it baby fat,
I made abstract transactions into fact, transforming weight on
  my frame into substantial mental gain
Gaining the respect of my teachers
I had learned the game inside out just by sitting on the bleachers
Work hard, Listen more than you talk, and doors will open

Niya McCray is a law student at Vanderbilt University in Nashville, Tennessee. She began writing poetry in the fifth grade and has not stopped since. In the past years, Niya has performed alongside poets in Vanderbilt Spoken Word during the annual showcase, at various events hosted by Southern Word, and as a solo performer for open mic and religious events. She believes that there is always an occasion for poetry but, more importantly, there is always a reason to let your voice be heard speaking words of truth.

CONSTANCE BYNUM, NIYA MCCRAY, AND ROMAL TUNE

The game is just politics
Take what you know and divide it by the number of people
    who can help you advance it
There's no way to make it sugar-coated or romantic
Don't forget that your peers can either hinder it or enhance it
Relax, remember that the enemy of your enemy is your friend
And you will need more than a couple of those to see you
    through to the end
But for those trying to remain invisible in plain sight, these rules
    still apply
Apply yourself,
Try to understand why x ever needed y,
Take the lyrical creativity that Common taught you, testify to
    your intellect, you too can gain respect
Count yourself as the more never the less
Strive to make your better its best
Me? I took words and molded them into things my teachers had
    never heard
They claimed it, said the words I held on to
Would launch me on a pad so supercalifragilistic not even Mary
    Poppins could stick with it
I intellectually slew the Goliaths that stood before me, with
    common sense and G-O-D
The ACT, SAT were both standardized tests designed to relegate
    me to mediocrity
But I'd been looking at this same twisted logic since I started
You have to learn probability: If Niya is a young black woman
    and no one else in her family has graduated from a 4 year
    institution, what is the probability that her choices will lead
    to failure, underachievement, or the systematic prostitution
    that we call just making it?

a.k.a. faking it, the answer choices are A. Likely, B. highly
improbable, C. none of the above D. too little information to
determine
But too often the information determines our fate before we
get there. And that ain't fair.
But if you're trying to even the odds you should conquer
Logical Reasoning: A student comes from a lower-class
family, Mommy, the sole provider, gets laid off. College
tuition is $58,000, subject to increase at the university's
discretion. How does the student pay for education without
debt, selling her soul, or losing both that dollar and a dream
that got her this close to her goal?
A. Not enough information, B. Impossible C. Possible with high
amounts of debt, D. none of the above
D because no unstandardized test of intellect or finance was
going to tell me not to be a better me
Kids with my mentality are as newsworthy as that red rose that
grew from concrete
I have my inner Machiavelli and I plan to build a foundation
brick by brick with knowledge
Nothing on earth was going to stop me from going to college.
Dear Niya, Congratulations on your acceptance to Vanderbilt
Congratulations on being closer to your dreams
I thought that I had reached the pinnacle of success or so it
seemed
Hard work is what begins after you touch the rim for the first
time
After you receive the audience applause for that super-hot
rhyme
The only failure is failing not to work harder, not to run faster,
not to learn something you didn't know.

CONSTANCE BYNUM, NIYA MCCRAY, AND ROMAL TUNE

Be better than you were to begin with, give yourself something
    to show
And let your inner motto blare with the savvy of Jay, the
    lyricism of Nas, and the individuality of the Cool Kids i.e.
I know I can be what I want to be, if I work hard at it, I'll be
    where I want to be
Me? I was ahead of my years, I was the one called upon to tutor
    my peers
To help the same ones who called me fat, black and ugly
Reminiscent of the B.I.G.
And I'm Notorious now for being lovely and having made it

Keiara's Beauty

Constance Bynum

When my sister was real young she used to ask me,
"Constance why am I so dark?"
and I would say,
"Because when mommy was pregnant with you she craved Oreos,
and she ate them so much that you came out chocolate."
She would think about the statement,
decide it was acceptable and continue doing whatever it was that
    she was doing.
As she got older and came to the conclusion
that Oreos don't have an effect on a pregnant woman's baby's
    pigmentation,
she asked the question again,
"Constance why am I so dark?"
and I told her "Because you're sun kissed."
She asked me, "Well what's sun kissed?"
I told her, "Sun kissed means that when you were born
you were so beautiful that the sun came out of the sky and onto
    Earth
just to kiss you.

Constance Bynum graduated from Middle College High School and is a student at Empire Beauty School in Nashville, Tennessee. She started writing with Southern Word in 2013 and has quickly become one of their featured performers at events. She represented the region at the Brave New Voices festival in 2013 in Philadelphia.

CONSTANCE BYNUM, NIYA MCCRAY, AND ROMAL TUNE

And as an effect, your skin became a little darkened
so everyone would know just how beautiful you were."
She thought about the statement,
decided it was acceptable and continued doing whatever it was
    that she was doing.
Now that she is older and knows the sun doesn't come out of
    the sky
to kiss beautiful babies,
and now that she knows her skin is darker than the socially
    accepted pigment,
she asks me,
"Constance am I pretty?"

The day a 12-year-old girl can take the views of society
and use them to conclude she is less than someone with lighter
skin is the day someone
somewhere
stands up
and says something
But because our minds have been poisoned
with society's stupid image of picture perfect,
our butts remain planted
and our lips remain sealed.
Who will stand up and start a change?
Our whole lives we have been told
the lighter the better
the thinner the better
the longer the better
the smaller the better,
so what do we do?

We wear contacts so that our eyes look brighter.
We take pictures in the light so that our skin looks lighter.
We wear heels and cut off our thighs so that our legs look longer
and smaller.
And we perm, press, and fry the heck out of our hair so that our
hair looks thinner.

But even Jesus had skin of bronze and hair of wool.
So when do we stop listening to the creations and start listening
to the creator?
When do we stop staring at our flaws and start seeing that we are
flawless?
And when do we stop listening to ignorant close-minded clones
and start listening to what we think of ourselves?
I'll tell you when.
It starts here, right now.
Because the fad of what looks nice is outdated and over used.
So ladies, the next time you see yourself in that mirror,
you tell yourself that you are beautiful.
Not because I said it.
Not because your mom said it.
Not because your dad said it.
But because God said it.
And the last time I checked he painted you not in their image,
but in his image of beauty.

MeetUp

Rhythm

Chapter 10

Rituals and Rhythms of Faith

Paul-André Durocher

In my younger years, I pursued a degree in music and music education, and my specialization was music education at the high school level. While I was studying and teaching music, I had several friends who were teaching elementary school music and many of them were using the Kodály method. One of the main things they would do was to have students intonate different notes and rhythms. It works well with a large group. Some students would be half notes and say "Toe-Toe, Toe-Toe" while others would be quarter notes who say "Ta-Ta-Ta-Ta, Ta-Ta-Ta-Ta" Still other children would be the eighth notes and say "Ti-Ti-Ti-Ti-Ti-Ti-Ti-Ti, Ti-Ti-Ti-Ti-Ti-Ti-Ti-Ti." And then there were the triplets, who would really mess things up by saying "Tri-o-la, Tri-o-la, Tri-o-la, Tri-o-la." Gradually, all the

The Most Reverend **Paul-André Durocher** (@padurocher) is Archbishop of the diocese of Gatineau, Québec, and president of the Canadian Conference of Catholic Bishops. He holds degrees in music, theology, education, and canon law, and has served as a high school teacher, parish priest, diocesan ministry coordinator, bishop, and archbishop. Archbishop Durocher is often invited to preach at retreats and to direct workshops in various areas of pastoral ministry.

different groups of students saying the different rhythms would be added to one another and it would sound beautiful, with large imposing "Toes," dependable "Tas," short and quick "Tis," and the funky "Tri-o-las." As these note exercises taught and gave rhythm to elementary school students, ritual gives rhythm to our lives and the lives of the young people in our faith communities.

Ritual as Rhythm

At its very basic level, ritual is a repetitious set of actions that fit together and give order and rhythm to our lives. For example, we can think about our morning routines (although I'm sure most of us don't call this a ritual). Most of us have a ritual that begins when we wake up in the morning. We usually do the same things in the same order every morning. For example, I wake up, get out of bed, put on sweatpants and a sweatshirt, and then head down the hall and turn on the coffee machine. Then I go for my iPad and download the day's newspaper. By that time I grab my coffee and I sit with my iPad at the table catching up on events. That's the beginning of my morning ritual. Eventually, I decide it is time to start getting ready for the day and I have to go shower. And even in the shower I have a ritual. I always start by shampooing. Maybe you have a different shower ritual, but I always start with shampoo. Once my head is clean I take a cloth and a bar of the same soap I have been using for centuries and I start washing the left arm pit and the left arm... and so on.

This shows the ways in which ritual shapes everything we do. And thank God for this, because I wouldn't want to imagine what would happen if we all had to wake up in the morning and think about every little thing that we have to do. "Shall I put my shirt on first or start with my pants? What does God want me to do? I'd better pray on this: 'Lord, I need to discern your will here.

Can you show me how to begin getting ready today?'" Thank God for ritual.

So there are small and short rituals, like our morning routines, that are like the eighth notes of our lives, going "Ti-Ti-Ti-Ti-Ti-Ti-Ti-Ti." They are so integral to our lives that we sometimes don't even know that we're doing them. These rituals are the rhythm that gives structure to our day-to-day lives.

We also have rituals that don't occur every day, those that happen on special occasions (like quarter and half notes), or those that come upon us unexpectedly and mix things up (like triplets). Just think of all the rituals that surround the celebrations of birthdays. People get together and celebrate with food and perhaps a few games. And then, at the end of the meal, someone brings out a cake with candles on it, each one representing a year of your life. These rituals are so common that we all know what to do when that cake is put down in front of us. We blow out the candles – but not before making a wish!

We have more rituals in our lives than I can even begin to list. And they are incredibly important because not only do they structure our reality, but they actually *become* our reality. Imagine what would happen if, on your next birthday, you check your Facebook page and not a single person wishes you a happy birthday. And then you go to work and visit family and no one mentions that it is your birthday. You would wonder what was going on. Maybe you'd think that there is a surprise party planned and waiting for you at your home. But then when you get home, expecting a large crowd of friends to be there, the house is empty. Eventually the day would end and you would be tempted to pull out your wallet and check your ID to make sure that you remembered what day your birthday was. And then you'd look at the calendar and see that it's today. But you'd wonder, did my birthday happen? Is it real? After all, the rituals are what make it real.

This is especially true when it comes to symbolic rituals, which are simply rituals that carry deeper meaning with them. Brushing our teeth may be a ritual, but it's not symbolic. But blowing out candles and sharing birthday cake *are* symbolic rituals. Making a wish and blowing out candles symbolizes the years that have passed in our lives and the hopes we carry with us into a new year.

The symbolic ritual speaks with a deeper voice. It has a more profound meaning. It speaks in a different way than language alone can speak – "Ta-Ta-Ta-Ta" and "Toe-Toe." In that sense, we might say that symbolic ritual is a language in its own right. It is in symbolic ritual that we enact the feelings and meanings that we may not have the words to speak.

One of the things I love about the Kodály method of music education is that it allows children to learn music together. It's impossible for one child to speak half notes, quarter notes, and eighth notes all by herself, let alone triplets too! So it's best to get a group of children to build a rhythm together.

This is like ritual in our lives. Some rituals, such as my morning routine, are done in private. But we also have shared community rituals as well, such as birthdays and graduations, baby and wedding showers, retirement parties, and national holidays and parades. Sharing these kinds of rituals creates and strengthens community, and structures our identities as members of a community. In belonging, we become.

Losing Ritual, Finding Ritual

For some people of faith today, symbolic ritual isn't a significant avenue for having and holding or expressing faith. But in Europe in the Middle Ages it was the primary way of expressing faith. One of the problems that the church in Medieval Europe was facing was that so many people had grown used to symbolic ritual that it had become detached from scripture, detached from the Word of God. The balance between scripture and ritual had become so lopsided that the latter seemed to overshadow the first, leaving scripture at the sidelines of faith.

Martin Luther recognized that this was happening. Being the good priest that he was, he felt that this was a significant problem. And so he challenged this. And when his challenge was rejected by the leaders of the Church at that time, he set out to continue to challenge and correct this imbalance on his own. And, in a nutshell, this is how the whole Protestant Reformation started.

The leaders of the Catholic Church, unfortunately, dug in their heels and continued to maintain this imbalance instead of learning from what Luther was saying. And while they continued to stick with ritual, Protestants continued to stick with the Word. Both sides ended up poorer because of it.

If ritual is like the rhythm of our lives of faith, then perhaps we can understand scripture as the melody. The rhythm may be fun, but if we don't have melody something seems to be missing. And how can we have melody if we don't have rhythm? Rhythm and melody need one another in order to make music live.

Rhythm and melody aren't all there is to music. There is timbre and volume, too. These also give music its richness. I suggest that these can represent ethical life and our commitment to the kingdom of justice, peace, and joy that Paul speaks about in his letter to the Romans. Building justice, peace, and joy around us – along with the melody of scripture and the rhythm of symbolic ritual – all of this combines together to achieve the fullness of the Christian life. And as rhythm, melody, timbre, and volume are common elements of all music across different traditions and cultures, so too are symbolic ritual, scripture, and the ethical life common across Christian tradition. So whatever Christian tradition we may belong to – Catholic, Protestant, or Orthodox – we all need to pay attention to symbolic ritual as being part of the symphony in which the movement of Christian life finds resonance with the rest of God's good creation.

Music and Young People

How do we do this? And how do we offer young people opportunities to engage in symbolic ritual alongside their encounters with scripture and their quests to live lives of justice, peace, and joy?

For one thing, we need to take time to explore symbolic ritual with the young people in our lives and in our faith communities. For churches that are liturgical in nature – like mine – this means not just enacting our shared rituals with our young people, but also exploring their meanings together.

Just think of all the meanings that are embedded in the symbolic ritual of the Eucharist. How many of our children have actually made bread before? Many of them likely have very little idea about how bread is made, joining the many of us who opt to buy our bread pre-kneaded, pre-baked, and pre-packaged. Imagine how powerful it would be to go and see how bread is made, to make bread with them, and then to break bread together. We could then reflect with them on bread in our world. In today's world, we cannot celebrate Eucharist with bread without thinking about the fact that so many people in our neighbourhoods, nations, and world do not have the bread that they need. "Give us this day our daily bread," Jesus taught us to pray. What does it mean to break bread in a world that is lacking food for so many? We need to ask questions like this with our children and youth.

And we need to go back to scripture to explore the meanings of bread for the Israelites, this manna falling from heaven. What does it mean that God would send bread to God's people in the middle of the desert? And what about the story of Jesus breaking bread with his disciples in Emmaus? His followers don't even know that it is Jesus who is sitting down and breaking bread with them. It is in the breaking of the bread that they recognize him, but not before he disappears. What does it mean, then, for us – tall or small – when we break bread and we recognize Jesus in this symbolic ritual, and yet he disappears? What does this mean for our lives? And how do we take these meanings and then go and be bread-sharers in the world?

These are the sorts of questions we need to wrestle with as we unpack our symbolic rituals. For those of us who are part of liturgical traditions, we need to unpack our liturgies, our rituals. For those who practise non-liturgical traditions, you need to get into it, to discover and start working and playing with ritual. By doing so, we invite young people to join us in exploring new rituals, new meanings.

Finding New Meanings

Let me describe this exploration for new meanings with a story. Not long ago I was celebrating the sacrament of confirmation with a group of young people. In the ritual for confirmation in the Catholic Church, there is a moment when the Bishop stands at the front of the church and leads the confirmands in professing their faith by renewing their baptismal promises.

"Do you believe in God the Father?"

"I believe."

"Do you believe in God the Son?"

"I believe."

"Do you believe in God the Holy Spirit?"

"I believe."

But before they profess their faith, the confirmands are to reject evil.

"Do you reject evil and everything that leads to sin and do you reject Satan, the Prince of Darkness?"

"Yes, I do."

This is the usual way in which the confirmands profess their faith before they are confirmed into the Catholic Church. But the only way to understand adolescent confirmation, then, is to understand baptism, which is what is being confirmed so many years later.

At the moment of a child's baptism, the priest gives the child and her family a candle, which he lights from a very large candle that is lit for the first time on Easter Sunday, reminding us of Jesus Christ, the light of the world. So the priest lights the baptismal candle and gives it to the child and her family, saying, "Receive the Light of Christ. And keep that flame burning in your lives." It is a beautiful symbolic ritual.

Once when I was leading a group of young people into the sacrament of confirmation, the organizers of this particular confirmation wanted to mark this moment with candles in order to symbolically remind them of their baptism and of the light of Christ that shines within them. So I handed out little candles to the young people before leading them in the profession of faith.

As I was standing there, I sensed the Holy Spirit passing through that time and space. She touched me with her breath and I was led to say, "You've got your candles. I'm going to ask you to reject evil. Do you know what evil does? Evil stops the light from

shining in our lives. Place your hands in front of your candle."
They all put their hands in front of the candles and the room
grew darker. I said, "I cannot see any of your candles anymore.
Now I ask you: Do you reject evil?"

"I reject evil."

"Do you reject sin?"

"I reject sin."

"Do you reject Satan, Prince of Darkness?"

"I do."

Then I asked them to bring their hands down from their candles
and to hold the flames up high. They all lifted their candles and
the room was filled with light. I continued:

"Now, do you believe in God, the Father, the creator of heaven
and earth?"

"I believe."

It was a powerful moment. The Word was, in a sense, made flesh
– tangible, real – in this ritual. We performed our faith and found
new ways to unpack this ritual together.

These are the sorts of things we need to do with young people
in our faith communities. And through their creative capacities,
young people can help us to discover new meanings in those rituals that shape the life of the church. They can help us to find new
ways of experiencing the rituals that have been passed on to us,
and that we pass on to them.

Ritual structures our lives as human beings. It carries the beat
of faith in our lives as believers. We should not be afraid of symbolic ritual. We can get into it with our young people, with our
children. Whatever symbolic rituals we use as we practise the life
of faith, let's creatively find ways to use and explore them with

our children so that these symbolic rituals become the rhythm that makes up their days, their weeks, their years, and their lives as they journey with Christ.

Chapter 11

Sacramental Youth Ministry

Alaina Kleinbeck

For many Christian traditions, the performance of sacraments in worship is a central practice of the church. But for those of us who serve in formational ministries with children and youth, sacraments aren't often given a substantive role in our ministries. We may teach about sacraments, and we may invite those with sacramental authority to celebrate them during worship services within our ministries. But often this is where the role of the sacramental ends. When sacraments are peripheral, we miss out on the transformative themes that a sacramental imagination can bring to our formational ministries.

A sacramental youth ministry is not a programmatic strategy that teaches sacraments over and over again. Rather, it's a lens for understanding what we are already doing in our youth ministries and why we're doing it in the first place. When we

Alaina Kleinback (kleinbeck.blogspot.com, @kleinbeck) has served youth ministries and organizations in St. Louis, Houston, and Norway. Before her current role as director of the Duke Youth Academy at Duke Divinity School, she was a director of Christian education working with middle school students. She is a committed bike commuter and novice gardener, both of which make Durham, NC, a good place to call home.

see our work with young people through a sacramental lens, our ordinary lives become filled with opportunities to see God's renewing and nourishing activity in the world. When we empower young people to make these faith connections between daily life and worship rituals, the sacraments become sacred re-enactments of God's daily presence in our daily lives; worship becomes far more than a dull, dry, and boring place to spend a Sunday morning; and the tasks and chores of everyday life become infused with deeper meaning.

For many of us in the Christian tradition, we see the sacraments as God's grace and presence being made known to the world through physical elements. Two principal sacraments, baptism and Eucharist, pour meaning into the acts of washing and feeding. Sacraments take the most ordinary and ubiquitous materials – like water, bread, and wine – and transform them into means of grace poured out on the world.

It's no accident that God becomes known to us through these ordinary, mundane elements. Throughout scripture, God shows up in surprisingly ordinary ways – as a stranger on the road, a still small voice, a fire in a bush, a baby in Bethlehem. To be sure, God also has a penchant for the dramatic, with commandment-giving and transfigurations occurring miraculously on mountaintops. But no one lives on these mountains. The people live in the valley where there is water for washing and renewing, and fertile land to grow nourishing food.

Sacraments are God's claim of presence in the valley – in our ordinary washing and feeding, affirming and forgiving, praying and partnering for life's journey.

The Mystery of Whole Being

When I first received training to work in youth ministry, I was exposed to Maslov's hierarchy of needs, a popular psychological theory used to understand the relationship of the various needs a person experiences. In the pyramid often used as a diagram of Maslov's theory, the meeting of physical needs provides the foundation for emotional, spiritual, and self-actualizing needs to be met.

Whether or not we subscribe to this model in a literal way, Maslov's ordering captures our imaginations as we think about the nurture and care of vulnerable populations – the young, the poor, the elderly, the sick. We often focus on the brute physical needs, setting aside the emotional, mental, and spiritual for a later time. For example, we ensure that everyone is fed as a necessity to be able to think at school. Similarly, we consider spiritual formation to be separate from physical needs. Congregations rarely focus efforts on the physical well-being of their members. In the same way that Maslov neatly ordered our variety of needs, we too discretely separate our needs and expect them to be met by discrete specialists.

But Jesus jumbles up our neatly ordered understanding of needs. We see this in his interaction with the Samaritan woman at the well in John 4, when he arrives thirsty but full of living water. On the other hand, the woman who seems to be able to meet her physical needs can't fathom how living water might quench her spiritual thirst.[1]

Jesus and the woman demonstrate for us something we know all too well: the relationship between our physical bodies and our spirits is a mysterious weaving, one that begins in our theology of the person of Christ. Traditional Christian doctrine holds that Jesus was fully human and fully God, yet mathematical equations seem too finite or fallible to illustrate the mysteries of the relationship between Jesus' physicality and divinity. In Jesus, the early church leaders urged, we discover an enormous mystery of divinity and humanity being woven together into one single being.

This mystery exists in us, too. Though human beings are mere mammals, our consciousness, ability to communicate deeply, and our spiritual yearning are woven together into our single being. We are body and spirit and mind knit together to create a personal being.

Sacraments replicate this mystery, weaving physical elements together with spiritual and divine presence. The very word *sacrament* has roots in the Latin word *sacramentum*, a translation of the Greek *mysterion*. Water mysteriously becomes and demonstrates God's renewing, resurrecting power. Bread and wine mysteriously become and demonstrate God's unending nourishing grace. Sacraments participate in mystery and help us acknowledge it within ourselves.

Rites of Passage

Many of us who are leaders in ministry with young people may already have a thorough understanding of the import of sacraments for our own personal journeys or for our corporate expressions of faith. But how can their mysterious weaving of physical and spiritual be an imaginative paradigm for our formational ministries with adolescents?

Baptism, a ritualized washing, serves as the church's initiation rite. In the early church, baptism was a serious undertaking, often preceded by months – if not years, depending on the place and time – of preparatory work. Catechumens, those interested in becoming part of the church, received instruction from church leaders on basic church teachings, transformed their daily lives

under the guidance of a sponsor, and committed to leaving behind the vestiges of pagan life in a liturgical practice called the
renunciations. For all intents and purposes, the catechumenate
was an apprenticeship program for new Christians.

The early church understood the radical transformation required of each person in order to follow the teachings of Jesus
and to participate in the full life of the church. Apprenticeship
allowed for individuals who were curious to try on the life, the
teachings, and the community, without taking on the full responsibility of burying one's self in the waters of baptism.

In congregational settings where confirmation plays a formational role, the history of the church's initiation rites can be
deeply informative. The catechumenate was the formational process of the early church to prepare novice Christians for baptism.
For young people who were baptized as infants, confirmation
often takes on this role, preparing them to make a confirmation
of faith; to take on a personal ownership of their roles, duties,
and commitments to the Body of Christ. Yet all too often, confirmation is simply a cursory and superficial activity, rather than a
life-transforming journey. What can we learn about faith and life
formation from the catechumenate's thorough and multi-levelled
approach to preparing a person for baptism? How can apprenticeship as a sacramentally minded task inform our approach to
youth ministry?

The ritual of baptism for catechumens was thick with sym-
bolism and meaning. She would have been stripped of all her
clothing and adornments, so to enter the water naked and free
from her pagan past. The water was not held in a small dish neatly
perched on a pedestal in front of church. Rather, it was contained
in a deep pool, often octagonal in shape to signify the eighth day
of creation – new creation in Christ. The catechumen was then

plunged deep under the water – buried even, as if buried in the tomb with Christ, dying to oneself and one's past life. But the tomb would take on womb-like significance when the catechumen emerged reborn in new life. She would exit the womb on the opposite side of the pool and was wrapped in white clothes. Then she was anointed with oil and given a bit of honey so as to taste the sweetness of this new life. And for the first time, she would then receive the Eucharist, communion with the Body of Christ.

In the preparation for and in the ritual of baptism, we can see themes of burial and rebirth, death and new life, renewal, washing clean, the sweetness of resurrected life, newness and re-creation, apprenticeship and community. A sacramental imagination attends to these themes and notices when we can connect the dots for the young people in our ministry.

Showing Our Colours

During a recent summer, I had the honour of walking alongside a ministry that seeks to empower young men, on probation for gang activity, to change their lives. The young men faced tremendous adversity and the juvenile street gangs promised a sense of belonging that, though profoundly deformed, gave them family, place, and purpose. For these young men, donning the colours of their gang was not simply pledging a fandom – it signified their being and belonging as much to themselves as to the world.

One evening we made pizza in the church kitchen and, while we ate, the leaders raised the possibility of getting shirts for the ministry. As the leaders asked the guys what it might mean for them to wear new clothes, these men engaged in a conversation that was steeped in baptismal images. For them, the shirts represented setting aside an old identity to take on a new one filled with fresh beginnings and hoped-for possibilities.

Many congregations are fortunate enough not to have to deal with the enormous task of untangling the self-identities and self-representations of their youth from a destructive gang identity. However, every youth ministry that I've encountered has shirts for its annual retreat, trip, or camp. And every youth ministry I've been involved in has grappled with connections between identity and appearance – these things are, after all, an important part of adolescence.

A youth ministry informed by a sacramental imagination sees this event-related, shirt-donning moment as an opportunity to talk about identity, about our belonging to a people, and about what our clothing communicates about these things. Suddenly a youth ministry T-shirt is imbued with meaning as it becomes an outward marking of a baptized community, a 21st-century adaptation of the white robes donned by the catechumens of the 4th century. When we talk about belonging to one another, something as superficial as clothing (and, no doubt, clothing is superficial) can become a symbolic reminder, a sign of a deeper reality.

Whenever we engage in renewing activities – in our personal appearances, on a service event or mission trip, in our neighbourhoods – we have in front of us opportunities to point back to God's baptismal promise to renew us and all of creation. We can peel back the layers of meaning infused in what we are doing and open up the imaginations of young people so that they, too, can see God's transforming and renewing work in everything around them.

Through the lens of a sacramental imagination, we invite young people explicitly to participate in the re-creative task of making things new in their communities, in themselves, and throughout the world. And when we have fun, as we are wont to do, we name *re*-creation as one key way in which followers of Jesus participate in God's re-creative work. Yes, a sacramentally minded youth ministry baptizes fun.

Transmuting Our Understandings of Justice

As the tradition of the church and theological themes of baptism inform how we consider apprenticeship and community, appearance and identity, renewal and recreation, the Eucharist has equally pervasive themes of grace, nourishment, and justice.

Even if consecrated bread and wine are unavailable or are not a part of our tradition, the power of holy eating can transform what we do as youth ministry. The holy eating of the community-focused meal, the Eucharist, is a radical act that claims that food is itself a means of grace. This claim has implications for our views of justice ministries and for our approaches to mundane tasks associated with food, such as choosing snacks and preparing meals for our ministry events.

Much like water is present throughout the world for washing and renewing, bread and wine are ubiquitous symbols of nourishment and provision. One of the greatest mysteries of the body and blood of Christ is that they do not run out. The act of gathering around a table set with simple bread and wine – Christ's body and blood – happens week after week, year after year, century after century, millennia after millennia. This simple yet profound act of faith remembers Christ's act of love, and feeds the communities through endless space and endless time. This miraculous feeding that does not run out ties our spiritual hunger to our physical hunger.

In Paul's first letter to the Corinthians, we see his scathing criticisms of the Corinthian church's classist practices at the Eucharistic table (1 Corinthians 11:17–34). The wealthy consume all of the food and drink, leaving those who already have less to go hungry. Paul condemns this practice, teaching that this meal is for the remembrance of Jesus – the Son of God who lived and died to reconcile God to the world. At the Eucharistic table, we remember that sacrifice and we are re-membered into the Body of Christ. At the Eucharistic table, all are fed.

The endlessness and openness of the Eucharistic feast informs the church's protest against the scarcity narrative that pervades our collective Western consciousness, showing up in our news cycles, obsessions with post-apocalyptic novels and films, and fear of welcoming strangers into our space and to our tables. When we drive to church on Sunday morning past places where the hungry live, we violate the spirit of the Eucharist. God's unending provision of grace and care compels our own ceaseless attempts to give (and to receive) grace and care in tangible and intangible ways. When our youth ministries engage in justice work, it is not simply to train "good people how to be less selfish" – it is to participate in God's Eucharistic vision for the world.

The tangibility of God's grace in the Eucharist informs our own attention to the tangible realities of our youth ministries. When I served as a congregational youth worker, food was present at every gathering. Despite rich possibilities for Eucharistic reflection, I saw the provision of food as an a-theological task, one that was equal parts functional (young people are always hungry) and marketing (young people are always hungry). I never considered that providing food, namely good food, could be an act of grace that gestured to the practice of taking Communion.

In a sacramental imagination for youth ministry, we ask, "What does the gospel taste like?" Our answers are contextualized to reflect the cultural influences and needs in our communities. We seek out food that tastes good to the eaters, that reflects a healthy stewardship of the land and the people who live on it, and that fits our budgets. We think deeply about what kinds of tangible nourishment will most faithfully communicate graceful love to the young people in our ministry. This work is deeply theological, deeply Eucharistic, and deeply important.

Transfiguring Our Youth

A sacramental youth ministry views its work through a lens that sees the physical elements and the mysterious and spiritual practices of the sacraments as foundational and formative paradigms for ministry. A sacramental youth ministry pushes every aspect of its practice – the use of space, the engagement of the senses, relationships, rituals – to speak theologically, as sacramental acts push us to connect materiality to spirituality.

These connections aren't limited to the sacraments of baptism and Eucharist and to acts of feeding and washing. There is a whole host of Christian practices that reflect the same mysterious connection between our physical experience and God's divine presence – traditionally, extending forgiveness and prayer to one another, giving affirmation to those in the midst of transition, and communally blessing the commitments made to journey together. These practices also include Christian hospitality (the creation of hospitable spaces to welcome our young and others, and making oneself vulnerable to being changed by the stranger), food practices (such as fasting and the love feast), speaking truth, engaging in justice work in our local communities, observing the Sabbath, creating space for grief and lament, playing music, creating art, playing, dancing, walking and running.[2]

When we help young people to recognize deeper meanings in everyday practices such as these, they become sacramental. Our time with youth becomes more than information dissemination and entertainment. Christian practices embody our teachings and bring our attention to God's presence in ordinary and unexpected places.

The lives of young people can be overfilled with busyness and expectations. The young people in our congregations may feel like they don't have time to build in one more thing. A sacramental imagination for our lives as Christians and in youth ministry is a way of empowering each person to mine their daily lives to discover that God is present in the lunch room, at sports and music practice, in the classroom and at work, in speaking against injustices and bullying words, at the environmental club meeting, and in taking a break. We walk alongside one another as we develop an awareness for the mysterious ways that God comes to us and makes us new, again and again.

The sacraments demonstrate God's desire and power to be with us materially and spiritually not only in moments on mountaintops, but in ordinary, valley times. We worship a God who is with us in the sacred and mundane, joyous and grievous, tempestuous and calm, fun-filled and boring. The truth that God is with us is not limited to our worship rituals and the sacraments, but is a truth for all times for all who follow Jesus, especially for young disciples.

---

[1] I first understood these connections in a sermon by Egil Svartdahl preached in August 2013, at Filadelfiakyrkan.

[2] See Dorothy C. Bass and Don C. Richter, ed. *Way to Live: Christian Practices for Teens* (Nashville: Upper Room, 2002).

Chapter 12

Village Vitality:
Cross-Generational Rhythms in
Ministry with Children and Youth

Anne E. Streaty Wimberly

Ministry with children and youth is a "village" or whole-community endeavour. It involves more than the young people and more than the efforts of the children's and youth ministry leaders. Whether this ministry centres on people of a certain age or stage in life, it's a frontline work of the whole congregation. Kids, youth, ministry leaders, pastors, other church leaders, family members, congregations, and even community agencies are all part of the multifaceted endeavours called youth ministry and children's ministry.

Anne E. Streaty Wimberly is Professor Emerita of Interdenominational Theological Center in Atlanta, Georgia, where she was a faculty member for 16 years. She currently serves as Director of the Youth Hope-Builders Academy, a theological program for high school youth. A popular workshop leader and lecturer, her latest books include *Youth Ministry in the Black Church*, *The Winds of Promise* (with Edward Wimberly), *Keep It Real*, and *Soul Stories*.

The nature of the congregation as a "village" is captured in the saying from the Akan people in Africa that was popularized in the United States by Hillary Clinton:[1] "It takes a village to raise a child." Use of the metaphor of "village" in ministry with youth and children is meant to highlight necessary patterns of communal solidarity, guidance, and support from which young people can develop a valued identity, life direction, and hope-filled ways of living in our world, which is ever-changing and often tough. However, the congregation as a Christian "village" holds particular significance.

As Christian "village," the role of the church is to assure Christ's welcome to youth and children in the same manner as Jesus did when the children were brought to him "so that he could bless them by placing his hands on them" (Mark 10:13, CEV). In fact, Jesus models an insistent welcome. His words, "Let the children come! Don't try to stop them! People who are like these little children belong to the kingdom of God," rang out in refutation of the view of children as a bother (Mark 10:14, CEV).

The congregation as Christian "village" also moves us beyond welcome to the intentional participation of youth and children. This stems from the recognition that children and youth have much to offer, as noted in the story in John's gospel of Jesus' recognition of the willingness and ability of a young boy to offer five barley loaves and two fish, and of the efficacy of that gift to feed 5,000 people. Jesus takes what this young person has to offer, blesses it, and then feeds the people (John 6:8–10). The essential message is that participation evolves from the understanding of young people as blessings.

As welcomed participants in the Christian "village," kids and youth are, in fact, both receivers and givers of Christ's blessing. In that "village," young people experience the kinds or patterns of relationships from which they come to know absolutely that they belong in community. Likewise, the community comes to know absolutely that without children and youth, real community ceases to exist. In this chapter, I will explore what constitutes a Christian "village" in the lives of today's young disciples. I will do this by sharing three key connected rhythms of this "village" that, I suggest, form a vital "village" dance: the rhythm of claiming the blessing of children and youth; the rhythm of mentoring; and the rhythm of intergenerational worship.

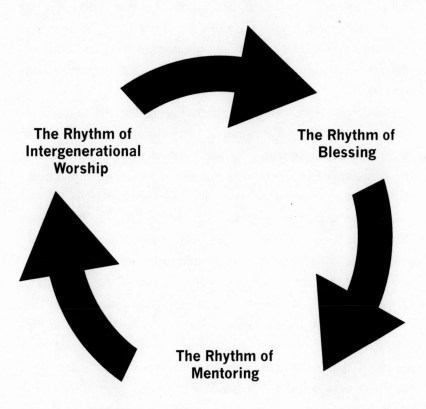

The Rhythm of Intergenerational Worship

The Rhythm of Blessing

The Rhythm of Mentoring

The Rhythm of Blessing

In *Keep It Real*, I point to evidence of adults' negative perceptions of youth and youth culture that result largely from problematic media portrayals.[2] These perceptions are also found in congregations, a reality complicated by a generation gap fuelled by youth-oriented interests, youth-developed language patterns, and ways of relating in peer relationships and social media. What emerges is the formation of a fragmented consciousness centred on competition, rather than on relationships that connect adults and young people, and separate places of functioning, including worshipping, that are deemed "necessary" and "right." Yet the generation gap can be overcome as congregations see and act on themselves as participatory "villages" where all, including youth and children, are received as blessing and where each has something to contribute.

 Blessing is about seeing the gifts of young disciples to the present and ongoing life of the church. Gary Gunderson calls blessing one of the "leading causes of life."[3] From this perspective, it is the very lives of young people that give the blessing. This understanding of blessing frames the efforts of the church as "village" to embrace and affirm kids and teens, knowing that in doing so the church becomes its better self. As blessing, young people also prompt the congregation's self-examination to the extent that it asks, "How did our kids become as they are? What about them do we recognize in ourselves? On this basis, how will we discover, name, and discern how to deal with what we find in life-giving ways for our youth and the whole village of which they are part?"[4] Underlying the search for answers is the absolute need for the congregation as Christian "village" not simply to receive youth as blessing, but for adults to be a blessing to youth and children.[5] Consequently, blessing takes on a dual inter-relational role that seeks the outcome of welcomed participation of young-sters on the one hand and life-giving, life-causing gratitude and responsibility-taking by adults on the other hand.[6]

Ministry committees, pastoral leaders, and/or groups of leaders and members would do well to recall experiences during their childhood and adolescence when they felt received as blessing. In the church of my childhood, which I experienced as a "village," reaching the age of 12 was an event celebrated through an an-nual ritual of recognition in the presence of the intergenerational worshipping community on the Sunday preceding the beginning of the school year. During worship, every young person with a 12th birthday that year was invited to the front of the congrega-tion, along with the parents or guardians and a senior adult. The pastor called each young person by name and after each name, the pastor – along with the parents/guardians and the older member – laid hands on them. Each adult described the youth's strengths, spiritual gifts, and talents, based on observations of and interac-tions with that young person within and outside the church.

The pastor reminded the youth of God's journey with them throughout their lives and about special qualities and abilities given them to be used to follow Jesus Christ in and beyond the church, as they strive to help others and make the world a place of hope. The pastor then told the youth that they would be invited to participate in opportunities the church would give them to build up their strengths, spiritual gifts, and talents; and they could also indicate their own ideas for these activities. The ritual ended with a prayer by the older member as the youth knelt at the altar surrounded by the adults.

The adults pointed to my gifts of music and teaching during my time of participating in the celebration. I was subsequently given responsibilities of playing piano for the children's choir, on occasion being the accompanist for the church choir and congregational hymns, and serving as apprentice during the adult church school class. Several Sundays later, I responded to the pastor's invitation to Christian discipleship by consciously choosing to follow Jesus throughout my life.[7]

The celebration was one part of the community's attention to young people. Church school, confirmation classes, and after-school group meetings for study, recreation, and service were common occurrences. Moreover, during the period of welcome in Sunday worship, the pastor intentionally drew attention to the kids and teens by acknowledging their presence, giving words of encouragement, and admonishing adults to be worthy Christian examples and guides for young people to follow. Predictably, the pastor also addressed young people directly: "God's got a plan for your life. Life isn't always easy. There will be some tough times. But know this: 'If God is for you, who can be against you?' Know that we're here for you as well! We love you!" Young people were recognized as contributors to the whole of worship. They sang in the church choir, ushered, read scripture, and offered testimonies or other presentations.[8]

The goal of a participatory "village" is to emerge from an understanding and practice of blessing. This goal was evident in what took place in the church of my childhood. The same goal is needed in congregations today and achieving it today calls for congregations "to simply be the Christian community Christ calls us to be, a community where every gift is exercised to its fullest for the glory of God."[9] Of course, this calls those of us who are adults to stretch ourselves beyond the comfort of our own culture by learning something of the language of youth and welcoming the ideas and stories of young people. Yet the key point is that intentionality in being with and on behalf of young people opens the way for them and the whole church to grow up in Christ. Indeed, the understanding of blessing makes possible acceptance of youth and children as gifts from God, emergence of new or renewed hope, and vital surges of faith.[10]

The Rhythm of Mentoring

Mentors provide a listening presence and wise guidance to others along the journey of life. They advance the rhythmic movement of relationships that make possible a vital congregational "village." In the Christian "village," mentoring invites shared stories, lives, and faith that open the way for faith exploration, affirmation, and growth.

We see mentoring relationships throughout the Bible, including ones between experienced mentors and less experienced, younger mentees such as Eli with young Samuel (1 Samuel 3:1–18), and the apostle Paul with Timothy, depicted in the New Testament epistles commencing in Acts 16:3. In the earlier instance, Eli's role as mentor was that of teaching Samuel how to hear, recognize, and respond to God. Paul's mentorship centred on equipping Timothy for ministry that would continue beyond Paul's own life; modelling before him and empowering within him self-assurance and competencies needed for his journey; fostering opportunities for his ministry experience and effectiveness; and expressing appreciation for the blessing of the mentoring relationship.[11]

The role of mentoring in the congregation as Christian "village" is an essential response to the needs and cries of today's young people for up-close, face-to-face care and guidance in this present technological era, in which persons are physically separated from one another. The web-based participatory world offers new and unfolding communities where people are physically

isolated from those with whom they are relating. These relationships have become an integral part of the everyday lives of young
people.

These web-based relationships, where people are physically
separated, present widening choices that append existing in-person, peer-oriented ones. Yet something seems to be missing in
these relationships – not only among young people, but among
adults too. In fact, Kenda Creasy Dean cautions that connecting with a community does not equate with communion. Even
though youth, kids, and the rest of us continue to rely on social
media and digital technologies to engage in community-shaping
activities – conversations, personal stories, thoughts, plans, and
pictures – there is an ache, a deep longing, for intimacy.[12] Her
view points to young people's search for a real and alive "village"
where they are known, where they fully belong, and where they
are active givers and receivers in its life.

When the "village" enters into the rhythm of mentoring, it
does so out of recognition of the yearning of young people for it,
and because of its potential impact on their lives. The important
point here is that a key rhythm of the church as "village" is getting
in touch with the craving of children and teens today for a safe
space and for a caring, guiding presence and listening ear; a space
where they can "tell it like it is" from the perspective of their personal realities and receive wise counsel. Children and youth have
many questions about God and faith; about who they are and the
direction of their lives; about how to handle family-related concerns, losses and grief, bullying and other types of violence; about
sex and sexuality quandaries, and other personal issues. Mentoring as a rhythm of "village" life offers opportunities for responsible and prepared adults to be travel partners in young people's
unfolding, storied journeys of life.

My experiences with youth, along with those of leaders in the Youth Hope-Builders Academy (YHBA) which I direct, reveal to me that young people crave the in-person presence and listening ear of caring others with whom they can engage in forthright truth-telling about the everyday "stuff" taking place in their lives. Young people further confirm this need by describing their experiences in a mentoring group or in a one-to-one relationship with a mentor. In YHBA, for example, a high school youth told of the death of his dad, and of receiving comfort and assurance from the leaders. He recounted being helped to hear and interpret God's direction in a manner somewhat akin to the assistance Samuel received from Eli. He experienced God speaking to him. But, for him, this word from God came through the leader's gentle questioning, "What is your experience of loss saying to you?" He told of the answer coming from the stories of others who seemed far worse off than he was, and he arrived at a point of saying, "It's not about me. God has something for me to do to help others." While in college, this young man volunteered as a mentor to young teens in an inner city, worked on justice issues as an assistant to a governmental official, and developed plans for law school.

In a mentoring program called "Faith Journey: Partnership in Parish Ministry Formation," for which I was principal investigator, a teen described her relationship with her mentor as an experience of "finding herself." She told of being able to "bare her soul" and of receiving affirmation of her selfhood and encouragement as a young woman to pursue her calling to ministry, in spite of discouragement from family members. Although her situation differed from Timothy's, the mentoring relationship that existed between her and her mentor contained many of the elements we see between Paul and Timothy. She recounted her mentor's "telling me that I have what it takes to become a minister" and "not to let anyone 'snuff out' the light that God has placed in me." Like Paul, her mentor recognized her potential for ministry and empowered her to see herself as a messenger of God. Her mentor also helped her find opportunities for service that would help her build ministry skills and clarify where and how these skills might be used.

It is necessary, helpful, and sometimes mind-blowing for mentors to take time to evaluate the mentoring relationship, to ask young people openly, "How are we doing? What are we doing that's helpful or not helpful to you?" On such occasions, the mentor might hear, for example, "WOW! You really did hear what I said!" Or, on the other hand, "Well, I guess I'd have to say that sometimes you talk a lot but don't really listen."

At its best, mentoring results in honest responses and testimonies. At the same time, it's clear that mentoring relationships invariably evoke the mentor's self-reflection and admission that the experience has an impact on her/him. This reality often results in mentors identifying their need, as one mentor put it, "to say what is in our hearts." Whether during times of open sharing by mentors or in written reflections, the heart's message, like that of the apostle Paul, is one of gratitude. As one YHBA mentor wrote, "My experience as mentor has been an intense time of remarkable growth. While I hope that I have been effective and have made a difference in the lives of my mentees, I believe that my experience with them has benefitted me the most of all. For this opportunity to grow while serving, I am greatly appreciative."

The Rhythm of Intergenerational Worship

Increasing attention is being given to the intergenerational character of congregational life, as a way of reflecting, to the fullest degree possible, the Body of Christ. This attention has emerged as more people recognize the age segregation that currently dominates much life in North America, including life in our congregations. The heightening countervailing movement builds on the view "that faith and spiritual development are especially nurtured as children participate with adults in teaching/learning/worshipping settings."[13] And it has biblical precedent found in ancient Israel's community-wide feasts and celebrations.[14] At these times, Israelites across the ages/stages came together to be reminded of their identity, God's nature, and God's activity in the past. Moreover, the early Christian church followed with intergenerational worship, breaking bread, prayer, and care.[15] Being together across generations is the mark of a vital Christian "village" that brings several blessings: reclaiming God's intent for shared faith; affirming together the value of all in the body; fostering support and teaching care for one another; creating special relationships between adults and younger generations and a space for passing on the faith from adults to those coming after them.[16]

Intergenerational worship is a primary space for these blessings to be deeply felt and claimed. Of course, this emphasis on "village" worship, where all ages are present, does not mean that separate age/stage activities have no place in congregational life. But it does mean that a blessing of inestimable worth happens when people of God of differing generations sing together, join hands in prayer, read scripture or litanies aloud together, and join God in repairing the world. But it is not always easy for congregations to ensure the experience of these blessings.

While, on the one hand, young people crave to be welcomed, affirmed, and engaged as active participants in worship, their critique is often that this experience is in short supply. Stark disagreements occur around music, dress codes, liturgy, and sermon topics and presentation. The voices of young people can call into question how we adults tend to structure our times of communal worship. The question of how to prepare for worship that responds to the needs and desires of youth and children is a pivotal one. In my estimation, there are at least four rhythmic movements that we need to reflect on when considering worship with young people.

1. Invitational Worship

Invitational worship takes seriously an intentional effort to receive children and youth in worship. It builds on the understanding that they discover the nature of God's welcome by how they are received in worship. Moreover, the meaning young people assign to worship depends greatly on whether they know deep within their bones that they are welcomed and wanted. Being intentional about reaching out to kids and teens and inviting them requires self-examination undertaken by worship committees who dare to ask the following questions: What do adults see when a young person comes into worship? In what ways do we receive them? How do we reach them and make them feel at home?

Likewise, it requires conversations with youth and kids and their responses to questions like, "What do you see when you come into worship?" "How would you describe the way you are received?" "What has been your experience of being invited to worship?" "What would being invited to worship look like to you?"

Intentional effort to reach out to young people and to invite them begins with open conversation with them. But it also entails creating an inviting space where they are seen, accepted, related to as worthy members of the "village," and receiving their concrete input for the content of worship experiences. Worship committees are immensely enriched by teen membership and welcomed voices. The powerful meaning of diversity in music revolutionized one congregation when, during a series of cross-generational suppers, their youth group and the adult participants were invited to share several of their favourite songs. Each was asked to precede their favourite song with a personal story about its importance to them. After the presentations, the youth taught the adults one of their songs and the youth learned a song taught by an adult. When asked to reflect on what had taken place, both youth and adults highlighted the power and similar themes of the stories that were told. As the result of the stories they heard, youth and adults alike told of deepening their appreciation for songs different from their own, and for the persons who shared them. This experience opened the way for the adults to welcome the young people's music and, likewise, for the youth to embrace the music of the adults. The experience of what may be called "intergenerational ritual interplay" became an ongoing part of this congregation's "village" worship.

2. Representational Worship

The term *represent* in the context of worship connotes a way of being the self and of presenting the gifts or talents one has for the good of the "village." Children and youth today are part of a seeing (sometimes called ocular) culture. Being seen matters. In fact, the glamourizing power of advertising media in consumer culture has a significant influence on shaping the public perception – especially with youth – that external appearance is pivotal to how we present ourselves.[17]

The engagement of youth in representational worship offers a countercultural way of shifting focus from their external appearance toward expressing their inner feelings and knowing of God.

Representational worship takes into consideration not simply the ocular culture in which youth live, but the expressive modes of communicating that are also emphasized among them. It is helpful, then, to create intentional places in worship where youth can express, through various creative media and in contextualized ways, learning and meanings of the Christian faith that would otherwise remain hidden. And through this expression, they also serve, teach, and encourage others.

3. Informational Worship

The intent of informational worship is to pass on the faith to youth and kids in ways that result in their saying, "I get it!" or "You've given me something to think about!"[18] Particularly carried out through sermons and songs, informational worship requires knowledge of the stories, views, concerns, challenges, needs, and hopes of the young people in our congregations. Making this happen requires intentional interaction with youth and avid insight into the media and experiences that are part of their everyday lives.

The intent is for the messages of the preached word and music to tap into the stories of children and youth, to invite their reflections on their stories, and to provide real answers to the tough questions of life, without denigrating or belittling them. Young people ask insightful and deep questions – How do I know God loves me when nobody else seems to? Why do I need to be Christian when my friends say it's not important? Why is there so much evil in the world? What does it mean to follow Jesus? – and they want help in finding answers to these questions.

4. Inspirational Worship

Young people become inspired by the worship experience when all of the preceding rhythmic movements – invitational worship, representational worship, and informational worship – connect together. They develop a passion for being present, participating, learning, and connecting with God and others in ways that are personally satisfying and transforming. When this happens, children and youth know deep within themselves that the worshipping "village" claims them as its own, and they come to know that God knows and claims them as God's own.

Keep Stepping

In the complex mix of moving into and through the rhythms of congregational "village" life, which assures the inclusion and participation of young people, we may find ourselves saying, as one leader I know once said, "What we are called to do is exciting and necessary. But it is surely challenging!" Yet amidst those difficult moments of stepping in rhythm, it is important to keep stepping, to get in touch with what has and is taking place that is promising and hope-filled, and to envision and reach for what must yet happen.

So let us keep stepping, remembering to celebrate what surely has emerged as blessings of God revealed in efforts to bring about vitality in the congregation as "village." Celebration is a spiritual discipline that affirms our intergenerational "village" connections, as well as our relationship with and reliance on God. An act of celebration is creating time in worship, youth groups, and special meetings to affirm or shout a unified "WOW" to the successes of our efforts with and on behalf of kids and youth. Through celebration, our intergenerational "village" also recognizes that every outcome has happened and will take place in the future by the grace of God. In fact, we celebrate God recognizing that celebration is one of the rhythms of God's people. We celebrate because we know that the blessings that come through what we do far exceed what we give.

---

[1] Hillary Rodham Clinton, *It Takes a Village: And Other Lessons Children Teach Us* (New York: Simon and Schuster, 1996).

[2] Anne E. Streaty Wimberly, *Keep It Real: Working with Today's Black Youth* (Nashville: Abingdon, 2005), xv–xvi.

[3] Gary Gunderson with Larry Pray, *Leading Causes of Life: Five Fundamentals to Change the Way You Live Your Life* (Nashville: Abingdon, 2009), 119–128.

[4] Ibid., 121. Gunderson makes the point from a family perspective by stating that "the blessings of children lead us to examine our lives in ways we never expected. Where did the 'problem child's' problems come from? If we look closely there is little in our children that we cannot recognize in ourselves, and the blessing of family requires that we find it, name it, work with it, and move beyond the boundaries of easy expectation."

[5] Ibid., 123. Gunderson refers to the "primal need to be a blessing to those who come behind us, and a deep sense of accountability to those who have come before."

[6] Ibid., 124. Gunderson refers to the formation of a dual consciousness resulting in "gratitude and responsibility that is life giving, life causing."

[7] The story expands on one in Anne E. Streaty Wimberly, "Worship in the Lives of Black Adolescents: Builder of Resilience and Hope," *Liturgy* 29, no. 1 (2014): 29–30.

[8] Ibid., 29.

[9] Kenda Creasy Dean, ed., *OMG: A Youth Ministry Handbook* (Nashville: Abingdon, 2010), 102.

[10] See Eugene H. Peterson, *Like Dew Your Youth: Growing Up with Your Teenager* (Grand Rapids: Eerdmans, 2000), 8.

[11] See 1 Timothy and 2 Timothy 1 – 4:8. The mentoring role carried out by the apostle Paul with Timothy is explored in depth in Stacy E. Hoehl, "The Mentor Relationship: An Exploration of Paul as Loving Mentor to Timothy and the Application of This Relationship to Contemporary Leadership Challenges," *Journal of Biblical Perspectives in Leadership* 3, no. 2 (2011): 32–47.

[12] Dean, ed. *OMG*, 83.

[13] The case for intergenerational faith and spiritual development is set forth in Holly Catterton Allen, "Bringing the Generations Together: Support from Learning Theory," *Christian Education Journal* 3, no. 3 (2005): 319–333. Further emphasis on intergenerational congregational life is found in Holly Catterton Allen and Christine Lawton Ross, *Intergenerational Christian Formation: Bringing the Whole Church Together in Ministry, Community and Worship* (Downers Grove, IL: InterVarsity, 2012); Vern L. Bengtson, *Families and Faith: How Religion Is Passed Down Across Generations* (New York: Oxford University Press, 2013); Peter Menconi, *The Intergenerational Church: Understanding Congregations from WWII to www.com* (CreateSpace Independent Publishing Platform, 2010); Mariette Martineau, Joan Weber, and Leif Kehrwald, *Intergenerational Faith Formation: Learning the Way We Live* (New London, CT: Twenty-Third Publications, 2008); and Howard A. Vanderwell, *The Church of All Ages: Generations Worshiping Together* (Herndon, VA: Alban, 2008).

[14] Allen provides documentation of intergenerational participation appearing in biblical texts on the Passover (Ex. 12; 23:15; Lev. 23:5–8; Num. 9:1–14; 28:16-25; Deut. 16:1–8; Ezek. 45:21–24); the Feast of Weeks (Ex. 23:16; 34:22; Lev. 23:15–21; Num. 28:26–31; Deut. 16:9–10); the Feast of Booths (Ex. 23:16; 34:22; Lev. 23:33–36; Num. 28:12–39; Deut. 16:13–18); and the Feast of Trumpets (Lev. 23:23–25; Num. 29:1–6). See: Allen, "Bringing the Generations Together," 322, 333.

[15] See, for example, Acts 2:46–47; 4:32–35; 16:31–34. See also Allen, "Bringing the Generations Together," 322–323.

[16] John Roberto explores the benefits in John Roberto, "Becoming Intentionally Intergenerational: Models and Strategies," *Lifelong Faith* 3, no. 1 (2009): 33–44.

[17] I describe representational worship in more detail in Wimberly, "Worship in the Lives of Black Adolescents," 26–27.

[18] For more about informational worship, see Wimberly, "Worship in the Lives of Black Adolescents," 28.

Chapter 13

The Great Imperative:
Why Re-Imagining Children's and Youth
Ministry May Be the Hardest – and
Most Important – Work of the Church[1]

Phyllis Tickle

It is almost always a good idea to begin a discussion like this with
a statement of the obvious, if for no other reason than simply to
establish a common ground from which to commence our conversation. In this instance, the obvious is that we are alive in, and
passing through, a strange time – a very strange time, in fact. But
the not-so-obvious thing is that while ours may be a strange time,
it is not a singular one.

Strange Times

That is to say that about every 500 years or so, Latinized
Christianity – or those cultures in which Latinized Christianity exists – goes through a mighty upheaval. Everything goes

Phyllis Tickle (phyllistickle.com) is founding editor
of the religion department at *Publishers Weekly*. An
authority on religion in the United States and a much
sought after lecturer on the subject, she is the author
of over three dozen books on religion and spirituality,
most recently *The Age of the Spirit*, *Emergence
Christianity*, and *The Great Emergence*.

"whoosh," to speak colloquially. And because literally all of society goes "whoosh," so too does religion. We are living in one of those semi-millennial eras, which is why so much of our contemporary context seems strange to many of us. It seems strange because it *is* strange. This era has a name – the Great Emergence. We, in the 21st century, are participating citizens of the Great Emergence.

Looking back five centuries from our time, that is, to the 16th century, we come upon another time of enormous upheaval – the Great Reformation. And if we look back five centuries before the Great Reformation, we witness in the 11th century what is known now as the Great Schism. And yet again, if we go back 500 years from that, we come to the 6th century and what is referred to as the Great Decline and Fall. And, sure enough, 500 years before the Great Decline and Fall is, of course, the 1st century, which brought about the Great Transformation or the Great Transition, for it enjoys two names.

Who knows why such periods of transition occur with this kind of regularity? No one. It's just simply true that every 500 years or so, for some reason, everything changes, and the form of religion that holds hegemony – that holds pride of place – changes with it. History is not prescriptive, however, though it is almost always descriptive. And, as intelligent people working in the kingdom of God, we have to pay attention to the fact that, for whatever reason, there has been a pattern. That is not to say that 400 or 500 hundred years from now our progeny will go through some similar tsunami all over again. I don't know that, nor does anyone else. What we *do* know and can say is that we Christians have indeed done this before…several times, in fact. Of course, we know a few other things as well.

For example, we know that the Great Reformation is always dated from October 31, 1517. Yet we also know that Martin Luther did not go to bed on October 30, 1517, as a good Catholic and wake up a raging reformer on October 31. It just didn't happen that way, and it never does. There's always a kind of lead-in, if you will. In the case of the Reformation, it is called the peri-Reformation. In our case, it is known as the peri-Emergence. But in any event, the "peri-" prefix refers to a period of about 150 years, give or take a decade or so, in which one can see the new, great *whoosh* beginning to build and build, until it blows. What is happening in that 150 years of peri- is the taking down or the disestablishing of the values and framework that had been the authority for guiding and governing life over the previous 500 years. That is precisely what we are doing – or actually are almost through with doing – now.

The peri-Reformation, then, was about the disestablishing, bit by bit, of the papacy, the curia, and the magisterium as the operative authorities until, on that fateful morning of October 31, 1517, our forebears woke up to a hard question. The question was as overwhelmingly complex as it was easy to articulate: "So now how shall we live? So now where is our authority?" It took our predecessors about 100 years to put a workable answer in place, just as it has always taken about a century to do that very thing in previous times of upheaval.

It now appears that history is going to say that the Great Emergence should be dated by 9/11. That is, 9/11 will be to us and our epoch what October 31, 1517, was to the Great Reformation. And like the people of the 16th century and of all the previous times of upheaval, we also have had our peri-, our period of about 150 years that have led up to our time of asking, "Where now is the authority?"

When we look around us, we readily agree that Protestantism has held hegemony for the last 500 years, in Latinized Christianity — that is, Protestantism has been the form of Christianity that has been most dominant. But what is it in Protestantism, many Christians are now asking, that won't quite work today? What is it that is, if not wrong, then at least is no longer quite right for many contemporary Christians? What is it that has to change? And even as we are saying such things and whether we realize it or not, we are birthing a whole new stream of Christianity, just by our asking. If you will, we are exploring a whole new tributary in the river that is Christianity. Thus, in 1517 when the Great Reformation came along, the church, or the river of faith if you prefer, more or less abruptly had a whole new tributary called Protestantism.

In considering those days, it is important to remember that Roman Catholicism did not cease to exist. In the same way, Protestantism isn't going to cease to exist even though today we are opening up a new tributary called Emergence Christianity. What we also need to realize, however, is that, aside from totally new converts, there is nothing to make Emergence Christians out of, except Protestants and Roman Catholics and a few Eastern Orthodox. As a result, the membership and attendance figures in Protestant churches, particularly, are falling and/or readjusting. That does not mean, however, that Protestantism is dying. It simply means that Christianity is once more growing and morphing into new ways and configurations.

War, Pills, and Changes Afoot

The second premise of interest to us today is that the Abrahamic faiths, of which Christianity is certainly one, have always been transmitted domestically. Always. Moreover, that transmission has always followed the same pattern of the tent and then the synagogue and then the temple. Or, if you want to say it in other, more familiar terms, first in the home, then in the church, and then in the cathedral. We, in our time and place as Abrahamics, aren't going to change that progression. All we are going to change is the context in which we follow it.

In this time of Great Emergence, as in all the other times of upheaval, spirituality changes, ecclesiology changes, and theology changes. And always there's a pushing back against that which held hegemony. Much of the pushing back for Emergence Christians is against doctrine, and against the lack of smells and bells and narrative. What Emergence Christians are looking for now (in fact, we could include the bulk of Christianity I suspect, certainly in North America and Europe) is active aesthetics and most certainly narrative. The cry, articulated in many ways, but with one intent, is, "Don't give us the doctrine. Give us the story. Not just the Bible stories, but also the stories of the Church. Give us our liturgy, if you will, and give us the richness of our tradition." There is good reason for that cry.

The Great Emergence, like all its precursors, was preceded by a peri-Emergence that can be dated rather specifically from 1842 and the work of Michael Faraday in field theory.[2] There are about four dozen distinct things and events that happened in the century and a half or so from Faraday to 9/11 that disestablished the hegemony of Protestantism and opened up new ways of ecclesiology and theology. From our point of view and in terms of the ideas contained in this book, the thing that mattered most, among all of those 40-odd changes, happened between 1962 and 1964: 1962 is the year the birth control pill was formulated, 1963 is the year that it was circulated for trial, and 1964 is the year it was released for public consumption.

First, however, it's important to note that what must be said about those years and the changes they enabled is not in any way a condemnation of anybody or any group of people. It is, rather, a matter of pure history that we need to look at, with objective eyes. That is to say that when the pill comes into general use in our culture, everything shifts. Historically and sociologically speaking, the major impact of the pill is not that it controls fertility. Obviously it matters greatly that conception could, and can, be controlled as a result of the pill; but that is simply not its most significant consequence over the long haul.

With the advent of the Second World War, we in this culture, for the first time in Western history, took good, established, duly married, respectable women out of the home and set them to working in non-domestic space. We called them Rosie the Riveter or Wendy the Welder, and we made cultural icons out of them, as well we should have. The only way Johnny was going to come marching home again was if Rosie left her kitchen and her ironing board and went to a plant in an industrial park somewhere, in order to throw rivets for ten hours a day, six days a week. So Rosie went to work because she had to.

But in the course of all this, she got some sort of teasing, tantalizing taste for working outside the home in a more convivial, less-isolated environment. She got a taste, too, for earning money instead of asking for it, and, almost as important, she got enormous social approval and reinforcement for what she was doing. These were all good things, of course, but cultural history ultimately trumped them. When the war was over, Rosie went back to being Mrs. Johnny, and we changed the names of both of them to June and Ward Cleaver. And that was all right, too, except that something else was afoot.

While Johnny was off to war, Rosie not only had an outside job, but she also had had their children to rear, one or two of whom usually was a female – which is what was wrong with June and Ward Cleaver as national images, by the way. June and Ward, alas, only had boys. Had they had girls, we probably would remember those girls today as having names like Betty Friedan or Gloria Steinem. All of this is to say that in the mid-20th century, thousands of young American girl-children went through pubescence while their fathers were away from home. What happened at war's end was that Daddy came home and suddenly the domestic dynamics changed. Now when one wanted something, one had to ask Dad. Mother could no longer give the yes or the no to things. They changed, superficially but tellingly, when Mother stopped whistling the way she had while Dad was gone. She had stopped because he said something about crowing hens and whistling women coming to no good end. Even more distressing, when Dad had not been around, one didn't hear raised voices and sometimes angry noises after lights out, etc., etc.

Thus we have our first generation ever of young girls maturing into womanhood and saying, "Not on my watch. It's not going to happen to me." So they got their college educations, and they got themselves paying jobs, too – but the jobs were as executive secretaries or office assistants or file clerks. How wonderful is that? How frustrating. We called it the glass ceiling, but there was a good reason for the glass ceiling. And now we must be anatomical.

The honest truth is that in those days before the pill and chemistry, women had no choice but to go through the menses every month. The reality of those times was that there was about one week out of every month when a woman was usually not at her most acute intellectually, when she was socially a little uncomfortable, a bit less poised, and when she was often emotionally labile.

But by 1964 when the pill is released, we have whole coteries of too-bright-for-their-jobs executive secretaries and file clerks who could avoid everything that came with menses by rearranging the schedule of their pills. And their bosses would be none the wiser.

And it worked. The glass ceiling began to roll back. By 1968 and 1969, and certainly by 1970, it was very clear that change was beginning to happen and that there would be no turning back. For the first time in history – and that's a broad statement – for the first time in history, so far as we know, the home is no longer the holding centre. Up until those pivotal years of shift, the man of the house had always gone out and conquered the world, so to speak. He or some of his confreres may have misbehaved at times, but, as a rule, most men had traditionally gone out and done their work for the sake of the home. All of what he did was, at its base, done for the sake of the home, and for his wife, who ran it.

But within five or six years of the pill, both partners are now going out to conquer the world because now they both can. The result, if you look at current statistics, is that over half of American households now have a female partner as co-earner, and almost a third show her as the principal earner.[3] There is nothing inherently wrong with this; it just is. And we must not judge it so much as recognize it for the major shift it constitutes.

The Tent Eroding

And we must recognize as well another reality in this shifting pattern: as both parents go out to work, so their two-plus children are going out, too. They are going for the next eight or ten hours to daycare or after-school care or some such thing. And when, as a family, children and parents all come back at the end of the day, they come back so that the home can restore them. The home – the tent – is no longer the informing centre. Now it is the place that restores us so we can go make a difference in the world.

When that happens, when it happened, one of the first things to get misplaced was family grace. That is not to say that families no longer sit down and quickly speak a rote grace of "We thank you, Lord, for this." Of course they do. It is to say that mealtime worship – that thing that happens when we sit down together and pray, adults and children alike, an honest prayer of thanksgiving and petition for mercy – got lost.

Another thing that went by the wayside under the pressure of changing times was the family altar. I am not suggesting that we no longer hear prayers in Christian homes; we do. There is a vast difference between hearing prayers, however, and having a time each evening when we all pray – parents and children together. When we "hear" prayers, though, what we really mean is that one parent listens to the children say their prayers while the other parent does the laundry. Yet realistically, if we are honest with ourselves, that very adjustment is almost necessary. After all, we have to go to work and school and daycare tomorrow, and we need clean clothes, etc., etc.

In the same way and for the same reasons, when we "read" Bible stories, we read them not from the Bible per se and not as member-tales from an overarching master narrative, but as brightly illustrated and self-contained quasi-myths rendered in grade-school language, and without subtlety or consequence. Perhaps even more debilitating is the fact that the natural telling of the tales of the faith – which once happened in the normal, everyday discourse between children and an at-home parent during the long afternoons after school and before supper – has also gone missing.

And so it goes, or so it has gone. It's that simple and that obvious. Gradually, bit by bit by bit, the transmitting function of the tent became, and has become, eroded. It's nobody's fault. It is a sociological change that has happened to us and to which we have yet to accommodate. But it also means that the tent isn't transmitting the habits of the faith as once it did. The tent isn't there telling the narrative or living the liturgy.

Mending the Tent

That is, we no longer have that keeping of the liturgical year that used to happen more or less naturally, when one parent was at home and the home/tent was the primal centre of faith. Yet if we can't get back to showing our children how to live the liturgical year – how to breathe the story on a daily basis, if you will – we are not going to prepare them, or their progeny after them, for the next 300 or 400 years of Christianity's formation.

I think there is a way to fix this situation, which probably really is what I intended to say in this, the final chapter of this book.

Christian parents of today's young children do not themselves – by and large and truth be told – know the stories of either their biblical or their ecclesial history. That is, they too were reared after the 20th century's interruptions. They too did not have the tent, and they attest to this with great poignancy and great longing, if and when the rest of us are willing to listen.

But those among us who are over 65, by and large, have those stories and formative customs deep within us. We – or they, as the case may be – still have them. I would to my soul that every congregation – every synagogue, to maintain our metaphor – might begin to contrive ways to match their seniors with either their own grandchildren or with other children in the congregation, or in the neighbourhood. Match them up so that the tent's narrative flow of faith – both read and enacted – begins to happen again.

If we can get our seniors deliberately and purposefully con-nected, either with their own grandchildren, which is an easy fix, or with other children, youth, and young Christians in the making; if we can get them connected so there is some kind of ongoing, sustained responsibility, then the tent can be restored in a new way. Listen to it what this may sound like:

"Mom, why have we got purple paper napkins for supper?"

"Oh sweetie, your Papa Joe dropped those by. This is the first night of Advent so we're going to use the purple napkins."

"Oh! Is that when we get those purple candles with the strange pink one?"

"Yes son, that's right. We are going to get those, too, because Papa Joe said he was going to bring some by tomorrow night."

"Okay, I think that's pretty cool. What's that pink one about? I can't remember why it's not purple, too."

★ ★ ★

"Mom. We're having pancakes for supper? I love pancakes! But why are we having them for supper?"

"Well sweetie, Mrs. Cavender from across the street brought over a new brand of syrup last night. She thought you'd like to have some tonight for your supper. Remember, she told you last week that we'd be eating pancakes tonight because this is Shrove Tuesday. And tomorrow begins Lent. She says that, in the old days, all of our ancestors had to get rid of everything before Lent started. They didn't have refrigerators or freezers, so they had to eat up everything that was good and that was going to spoil over the next 40 days. So they made pancakes. We're doing it because our people have been doing it for centuries. She says we're doing it because this is how we prepare and acknowledge the coming of Easter."

★ ★ ★

"Why do those rolls have sugar criss-crossed on 'em?"

"They're hot cross buns, kiddo. Miss Edith brought them over a few minutes ago."

"Hot cross buns. Why?"

"This is Good Friday. This is the day Jesus was crucified on a cross, more or less like the ones on our rolls. We remember by eating hot-cross-buns."

"Oh, God!"

"Precisely!"

And so it goes. And so it has gone for centuries, until our recent interruption. The transmittal of the faith within the tent – this is the thing we must find a way within our different and strange time to return to. The Great Emergence and those Christians who are forming it cry out to us for the tent. Let us show them how, under different social and cultural circumstances, to establish it again.

Let me add one last thing. Paul's second letter to Timothy is fascinating and I think we don't listen to it as much as we should. Paul and I have some trouble from time to time, but there's no question that he is right about this. He greets Timothy and then he says, "I'm reminded of your authentic faith, which first lived in your grandmother Lois and your mother Eunice. I'm sure that this faith is also inside you" (2 Timothy 1:5, CEB).

Perhaps we are spending too much time looking for Timothys and not enough time looking for the Loises and Eunices, who are going to form the Timothys.

I would submit that unless those of you who are workers in the vineyard can solve, or help the rest of us solve, this problem, we and those who come after us are going to be in great distress of heart and mind. I do not envy you your job, but I do most surely pray for you. In so many ways, the next four centuries of Christianity rest in your hands, not just in what you do with your congregants and their children, but how you can make that spread out into the wider world of the unchurched and the no-longer churched.

May God bless you always in that endeavour.

---

[1] This chapter is revised from the transcription of the presentation I delivered at Faith Forward 2014.

[2] Michael Faraday is best known to most Americans as a character on "LOST," a notoriety he earned because of his 19th-century work as a "chemist," though we would more accurately refer to him today as a physicist. By any category title, he was a brilliant man whose skills led him to run the gamut from doing practical things in applied science – like the invention of the Bunsen burner, for example – to developing the formulae that identified and codified the principles of field theory, upon which essentially all of contemporary electrical systems and much of contemporary physics rest.

[3] Women in the Labor Force: A Data Book. http://www.bls.gov/cps/wlf-databook-2013.pdf.